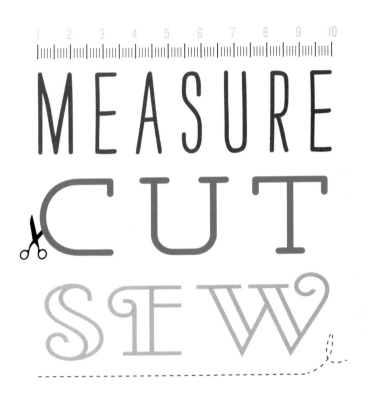

MEASURE CUT SEW

PATTERN-FREE PROJECTS USING SIMPLE SHAPES

by Susan Wasinger

LARK
New York

New York

An Imprint of Sterling Publishing
1166 Avenue of the Americas
New York, NY 10036

ISBN 978-1-4547-0907-7

Distributed in Canada by Sterling Publishing
c/o Canadian Manda Group, 664 Annette Street
Toronto, Ontario, Canada M6S 2C8
Distributed in the United Kingdom by GMC Distribution Services
Castle Place, 166 High Street, Lewes, East Sussex, England BN7 1XU
Distributed in Australia by Capricorn Link (Australia) Pty. Ltd.
P.O. Box 704, Windsor, NSW 2756, Australia

For information about custom editions, special sales, and premium and
corporate purchases, please contact Sterling Special Sales at 800-805-5489 or
specialsales@sterlingpublishing.com.

Manufactured in China

4 6 8 10 9 7 5 3 1

larkcrafts.com

MEASURE
CUT
SEW

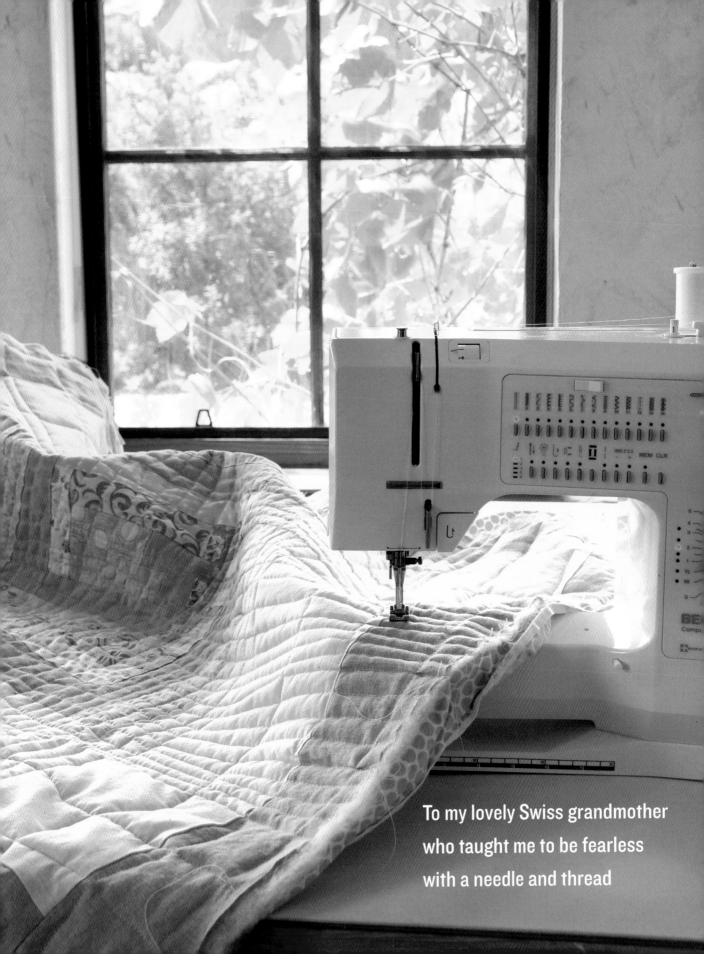

To my lovely Swiss grandmother
who taught me to be fearless
with a needle and thread

MEASURE CUT SEW

Contents

Why this book?

I LOVE SEWING, BUT I HATE PATTERNS

The projects in *Measure Cut Sew* do away with the wrestling and the struggling, the mind-numbing figuring, the hand-cramping finagling that complex sewing patterns have traditionally asked of us. There are no patterns to buy, no templates to print out, and no rune-like markings to decode. *Measure Cut Sew* uses the simplest geometric shapes that are easy-to-measure and easy-to-cut, but turn into easy-to-sew sophisticated, clever, fetching projects. Who knew that you could make a fashionable, light-weight blazer from 6 simple rectangles? Or what about a travel kit that's not much more than 2 squares, 1 zipper, and a clever turn or two? Only the construction is simple, the design is smart, and slick, and sassy. Just measure out the dimensions, make a few cuts, then get sewing.

100%

PATTERN-FREE SEWING

All the projects are made using measurements and instructions, no patterns or templates allowed

24+

FUN, FUNCTIONAL PROJECTS

Sew beautiful and useful clothing, accessories, home decor, stuff for kids, gifts for all . . .

It's pretty astounding actually, how much shape and dimension you can coax from a flat piece of cloth...

3 EASY-DOES-IT STEPS

easy measure, quick cuts, simple sew

side pieces **(cut one)**

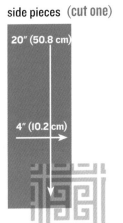

20" (50.8 cm)

4" (10.2 cm)

center pieces **(cut one)**

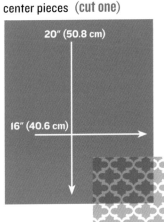

20" (50.8 cm)

16" (40.6 cm)

top pieces **(cut two)**

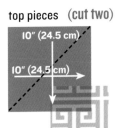

10" (24.5 cm)

10" (24.5 cm)

Measure

2   3

Easy-to-follow
simple-to-fathom
dimensions on every piece

Cut

Straight-forward cuts
very few curves
no confusing symbols

Sew

Useful how-to photos
intelligent construction
savvy design

How to measure up . . .

Cutting a square is a cake walk. Falling-off-a-log simple. Why do we even need to discuss it? Well, as easy as it is, there are a few tips and tools that can make it even easier. To make measuring and figuring as easy as possible all seams in the book are ¹/₂″ (1.3 cm) (unless otherwise specified).

Here are the tools that you will need to ensure that everything is perfectly made to measure.

A FLAT RULER OR YARDSTICK is best when you are measuring an expanse of flat fabric. Most of the time, an 18″–24″ (45.7–61 cm) ruler is going to be just fine. Occasionally, a longer length could be helpful. Consider having a yard stick handy to use for those longer expanses of fabric.

A STRAIGHT EDGE (which could *also* be your ruler) helps you draw a straight cutting line on your fabric. You want it to have a nice smooth edge so the marker or pencil runs along it without dips or jumps.

A MEASURING TAPE (also called a tailor's tape) is soft and flexible— often made of cloth—it allows you to measure the distance around things and measure a variety of things that are not flat. Like waists for instance, or head circumference. Also, it allows you to take longer measurements without having to deal with a really long and unwieldy ruler or stick.

A PLASTIC DRAFTING TRIANGLE is the perfect tool for making a square corner or 90 degree angle. It doesn't have to be a huge one as you can line up a longer ruler with one of the edges, thus extending the reach of the perpendicular line.

THE FEW CIRCLES that are used in this book are all cut out with the help of glassware and crockery. To be specific, the smaller circles mostly were traced with mugs or juice glasses, larger circles were traced with the help of a salad plate. I realize a compass is the more sophisticated tool for drawing circles, but I think it is quicker and easier to just use something circular you already have on hand.

Jar lids, flower pots, soup cans, and salad bowls could also do the job.

USE A MARKER that is easiest for you to see, use, and clean away, I'm partial to the use of a pin or a disappearing ink fabric marker myself as those two work for me in 90% of cases. However, there are fabrics, like black canvas, that no marker can mark. In those cases, have an alternate handy like a chalk or fabric marking pencil.

WORK THE SELVAGE. The selvages are the fabric edges that are part of the weaving process. They are more tightly woven, non-raveling edges that often have writing or a line of color running up the side. Those are perfectly straight, uncut edges and can be trusted as "square" and straight. Selvages are your friend. Use them as your straight side and then use a 90 degree triangle tool to ascertain the lines perpendicular to the selvage to make that perfectly square corner. Unlike the selvage, the cut end of a fabric is **NOT** guaranteed to be straight, so the selvage is your key to cutting things straight with the grain of the fabric.

Look sharp!

a few tips on marking and cutting your projects

How hard can it be, cutting a lot of straight lines?

Truth is, not hard at all! That is one of the many wonders of these projects, no incredibly

fussy pattern pieces to wrestle with. No impossibly complex curves to navigate.

Still, here are a few things to think about before you dive in

(because the point of this whole book is that you just get to dive right in!).

1

Consider *not* cutting all the pieces all at once, but rather cut-as-you-go so that adjustments can be made as to size and fit and design. I always disliked the tyranny of every seam having to be exact lest you run over or under with the next piece that comes along. Now is your chance to cut pieces to fit. Even better, waiting to cut pieces until I need them lets me hold out until the bitter end to decide on final colors or prints, something that makes the entire sewing experience more of a design process and less of a dull engineering challenge.

2

The amount of fabric specified in the instructions is a rough estimate and pretty universally generous. Fabric widths vary, patterns, prints, stripes, and stretchiness can all dictate the direction things need to be cut. So, I thought ample extra fabric, the more the merrier. Because every project states up front the dimensions of the pieces you will cut, you can do the math yourself. Base it on the fabric you want to use, and you can create more precise estimates of fabric needed. I won't be offended if you buy less fabric than I specified.

3

As for cutting tools, I'm a scissor person myself, but I can see the value of getting cozy with a rotary tool and cutting mat. Because most of the projects in this book are based on rectangles, a rotary tool is going to feel right at home here. Whatever you're most comfortable with, that is the right tool to use.

Don't be caught without a small pair of thread scissors or nippers. Stay on top of snipping off those threads at the end of a seam. It keeps your work clean and tidy and makes you look like you know what you're doing.

4

Invest in one of those disappearing markers you can buy at the fabric store. Wait, Freudian slip. The markers aren't disappearing, but the marks you make with them are supposed to disappear overnight or more quickly if you wipe them with a damp cloth. Come to think of it, the markers themselves are always disappearing in the numerous black holes that dot my studio landscape. Maybe you should buy two . . . They are great for scribing a cutting line or tracing a shape. Or marking a spot. Test the pen on a scrap of your fabric first to make sure the marks do disappear completely.

5

Of course you've heard the saying, "measure twice, cut once." But I'd like to propose an amendment. Mine would insist you "measure thrice." It takes 30 seconds to check and recheck your measurements. It does *not* take 30 seconds to drive to the fabric store to buy another couple yards to start all over again . . .

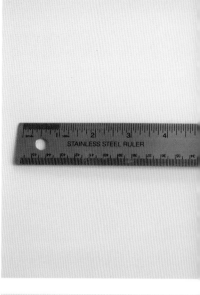

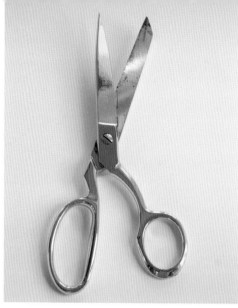

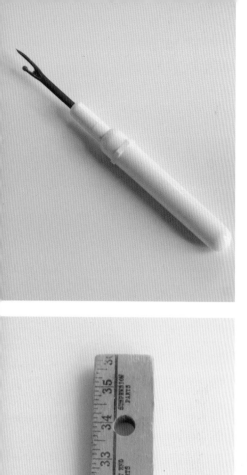

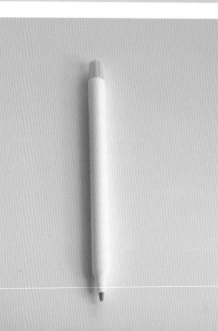

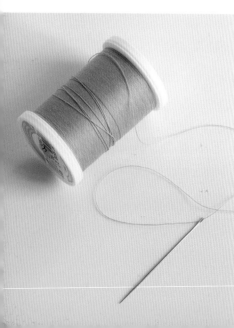

So, start sewing

⋙ This book expects you to know the basics of how to sew. How to use your machine, how to make a seam, how to speak the basic vocabulary. The projects are sewn mostly on machine, but there is a little bit done by hand. You have to know a stitch or two or at least be able to google your way through an unfamiliar one.

⋙ Years of fearless trial and error has taught me that you can sew most any kind of fabric with almost any home sewing machine including leather, heavy canvas, knits, upholstery fabrics, odd things you've never heard of like buckram. Get the right needle, and don't be afraid to swap them out on your machine. The needle that works beautifully on silk, doesn't do the trick on leather. But a leather needle, when its needed, is an absolute revelation.

⋙ I have a box of different presser feet for my machine. Don't understand 90% of them. But I do love my zipper foot when the occasion calls for sewing something off-center.

⋙ My best sewing advice is to go slow and steady, use lots of pins, but remove them before you sew over one, occasionally baste. That machine needle moves fast, keep your fingers and toes out of the way. Never fear hand-stitching. Some things demand it. Its precise, and useful, and it can feel like meditation in our loud, dizzyingly fast world.

⋙ Keep your thinking cap on at all times. You might have a better idea of how to do something than I do. Sewing is domestic engineering. It is drawing with fabric and thread. It will make you a better spatial thinker. And it will remind you that your hands have wisdom that your brain doesn't yet know. Trust, and play, and look at the pictures, and don't be afraid to pull out the seam ripper if you don't get it right the first time.

YOUR ESSENTIAL SEWING KIT

Keep it handy. Its loaded with the must-have tools that will get you through the projects in the book.

sewing machine

measuring tape

yard stick

metal or plastic straight edge

straight pins

scissors

seam ripper

marking pen, pencil, or chalk

thread

hand-sewing needle

optional rotary tool

optional cutting mat

How to create shape
with tucks, pleats, gathers, and gussets . . .

It seems an audacious idea to start a book full of sewing projects with nothing but a few unpromising-looking rectangles, the occasional triangle, a smattering of circles. But there is magic in all those simple shapes. The trick is to add dimension with changes of plane, to go beyond the x, y axis and add the z. What tucks, pleats, gathers, and gussets all have in common is they are a seam that changes the direction of a fabric and causes it to jump into a third-dimension. This little seam gives structure and volume and form to something flat and straight and shapeless. Here are a few of the very best shape-shifters:

MAKE GUSSETS

A horizontal seam that bisects a vertical seam, creating a kind of structural crossbeam that opens and expands the shape from flat to three dimensional.

USE PINTUCKS

A series of small, folded seams that run parallel to one another decreasing the width of fabric dramatically in one area, gracefully segueing into a dramatic, frothy increase in volume where the tucks end.

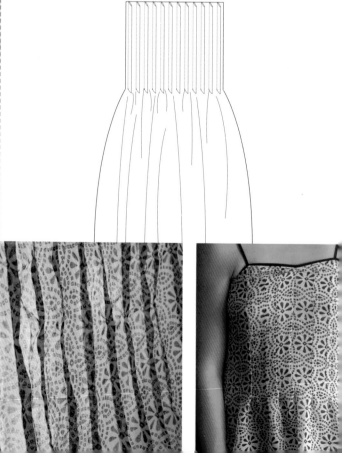

FROM FLAT TO FULLY FORMED

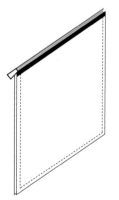
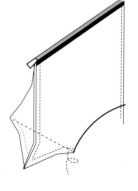

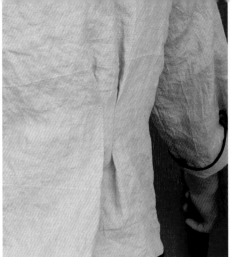
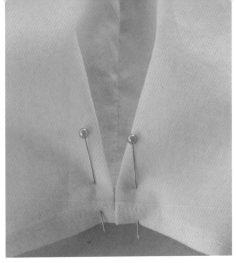

SEW PLEATS

Folds that create a narrowing in of an otherwise straight fall of fabric. Pleats can be a short length of seam within an otherwise flat piece of fabric or they can be folds that are loose and open but secured down on one end with stitching. The effect always includes a nipping in at the point of the pleat, but also a flaring out at the point the pleat ends.

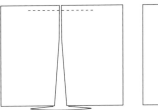
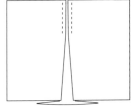

pleats create fit in one place and flare in another

a sample pleat cross-section

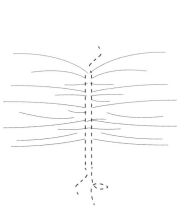

one or two lines of extra-long length stitches are used for gathering. The top thread of the machine stitch is then pulled to bunch up the fabric into tiny folds

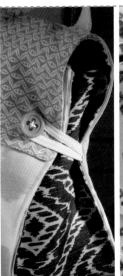
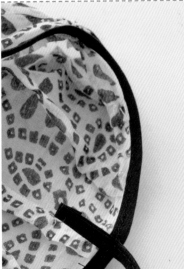

GATHER & CINCH

Gathers refer to fabric that is literally gathered up, squeezed, or compressed so it takes up less space resulting in soft, slightly chaotic folds and tucks that puff up further away from the gathering point. Cinching is a form of wrapping or belting something to minimize its size, resulting in a narrowing in one area and a shapely flaring out in another.

Material concerns
it's the little details that make it your own . . .

It really is uncanny how a shot of color, a surprising fabric, a brazen button, a brassy zipper can transform a simple project into something to obsess over, to project on, to fall in love with. Sometimes it seems there is nothing to find in all the garish plenty of the big box fabric stores, everything seems predictable and expected. But, dig a little deeper, there are treasures hiding in plain sight. Combine fabrics in unexpected ways, look for the notable notions, be fearless with hardware. But also, scour online sites for unexpected pieces and parts. Use stuff from your stash. Buy the good stuff whenever you can. Quality materials really do make something better. And they honor the time and energy you invested in the project.

Here are a just few things worth tracking down:

heavyweight canvas
raw and adventurous

natural linen
organic and real

wool weaves felted in the washing machine
soft and scrumptious and fray-free

utility fabrics like ticking, waffle toweling, buckram
wonderfully weird

a little bit of leather
to keep things real

vintage pieces of embroidery or ribbon
make it one-of-a-kind

metal hardware and heavyweight zippers
no-nonsense industrial design

brightly-colored foldover elastic
beauty, utility, and pop

outdoor fabrics
built in toughness, endless style

the finer cottons
cotton lawn, voile, batiste, challis, chiffon—they're worth searching for

calico scraps/stash
horde multiple prints in analogous colors

cords, ribbons, tapes and webbing
seek the unusual–buy it if you like it even if you don't yet know where you'll use it yet

Nantucket TUNIC

Sew this breezy top in no time flat for your next trip to the beach. A bit of borrowed embroidery from vintage linens does all the hard work for you to make this simple design sublime.

EASY HARD
gauge of difficulty

Comes in two sizes: extra small/small and medium/large
(please see page at right for size conversions)

MATERIALS

2 yards (1.8 m) lightweight
cotton 44-inches (111.8 cm)
wide, like seersucker

2 vintage, embroidered
pieces with decorative edges

thread

TOOLS

sewing kit *(see page 15)*

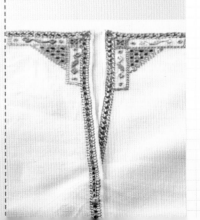

MEASURE & CUT

front sides (cut two)
24″, 26″ (61, 66 cm)

back (cut one)
24″, 26″ (61, 66 cm)

center front (cut one)
15″, 16″ (38.1, 40.6 cm)

8″, 9″ (20.3, 22.9 cm)

20″, 23″ (50.8, 58.4 cm)

8″, 9″ (20.3, 22.9 cm)

✂ cut from seersucker

sleeves (cut two)
19″, 20.5″ (48.3, 52.1 cm)

yoke (cut two)
10″, 11″ (25.4, 27.9 cm)

3.5″, 4″ (8.9, 10.2 cm)

18″, 19.5″ (45.7, 49.5 cm)

✂ cut from embroidered piece

Sizing for extra small/small and medium/large

ASSEMBLE

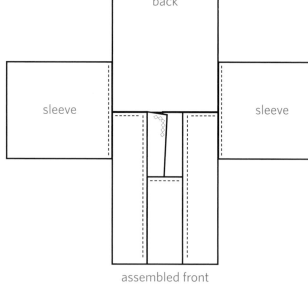

sleeve

back

sleeve

assembled front

One of the fun things about this tunic is the use of vintage embroidery for a unique detail at the yoke. I used decorative linen napkins from the 50s found at a junkstore for about $1. Antique napkins, embroidered handkerchiefs, or lacy guest towels are all good choices. Look for pieces that have a pretty edge detail, as that will become the placket edge and the neckline. They also need a nice intricate corner detail to become the collar. Be sure to look at both sides of the embroidery as when the color falls open, you will see the "backside" of the piece.

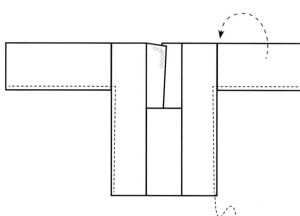

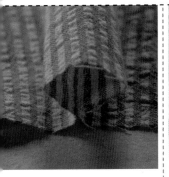

1 PLEATS At the center of both the center front piece and the back piece is a simple pleat that adds volume and shape to the garment. Determine the center of each piece and fold in half along the center line. One inch in from the fold line, sew a short seam 2" (5.1 cm) down from the top.

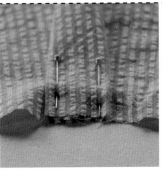

2 PRESS THE PLEATS Press the sides of the pleat flat on the back side and pin. Be sure the two sides are equal relative to the center line. Baste down with a line of stitching.

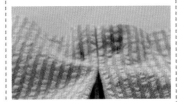

3 MAKE YOKE Cut out your yoke pieces, saving the interesting edge and corners for the side that will become your neckline (top, corner, and side). Overlap the bottom edge of the embroidered pieces about ½" (1.3 cm) and pin to hold.

4 CENTER PANEL AND SIDES With right sides together, pin the yoke and the center panel together, aligning the centers. Sew, then press open.

5 SEW SIDE SEAMS With right sides together, pin front side panels to the center panel along the long axis on each side. Sew.

6 SEW SHOULDER SEAMS. Pin the front to the back at the top with right sides together. This shoulder seam will run from the edge of the yoke (where the embroidered piece begins) to the side edge of the front and the back panels as shown.

7 ATTACH SLEEVES. Find the center of the sleeve and line it up with the shoulder seam. With right sides together, pin the sleeve piece to the front and back pieces as shown. Sew the sleeve in place.

Finish the collar back by folding down the raw seam edge ¼" (6 mm) then ¼" (6 mm) again. Hand or machine stitch to finish.

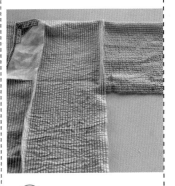

8 SEW ARM AND SIDE SEAMS. Fold the front and back pieces down at the shoulder seam so the right sides are together. Line up the front sides with the back sides. Line up the front of the sleeve with the back of the sleeve. Pin. Sew up the side from the bottom to make the side seam. Make a 90-degree turn at the underarm, and sew the sleeve together.
To finish: make a 1" (2.5 cm) rolled hem at the bottom of the shirt, and the sleeves.

Zipper Pocket TOTE

This smart silhouette adds a lot of attitude to your wardrobe. It gets style points from a few carefully positioned zippers, handles, and a simple gusset that takes it quickly from square to shapely.

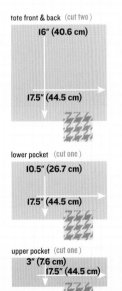

Finished size 16" x 12" x 3" (40.6 x 30.5 x 7.6 cm) (not including handles)

MATERIALS

1 yard (91.4 cm) upholstery-weight fabric 44-inches (111.8 cm) wide

½ yard (45.7 cm) pretty/ soft/colorful micro-suede for the lining

½ yard (45.7 cm) medium to heavyweight fusible interfacing

one 16-inch (40.6 cm) medium to heavyweight, non-separating metal zipper in black

two 7-inch (17.8 cm) jeans or pocket metal zippers in black

pair of sew-on leather handles (with pre-drilled holes)

18'' (45.7 cm) of ½-inch (1.3 cm) wide grosgrain ribbon in black

3 heavyweight jump rings for zipper pulls

thread to match outer fabric

thread to match lining

thread to match handles and pulls

TOOLS

zipper foot (for your sewing machine)

thimble

iron

needle-nose pliers

sewing kit (see page 15)

MEASURE & CUT

tote front & back (cut two)
16" (40.6 cm)
17.5" (44.5 cm)

tote lining (cut two)
16" (40.6 cm)
17.5" (44.5 cm)

lower pocket (cut one)
10.5" (26.7 cm)
17.5" (44.5 cm)

upper pocket (cut one)
3" (7.6 cm)
17.5" (44.5 cm)

iron-on interfacing (cut two)
15.5" (39.4 cm)
17.5" (44.5 cm)

ATTACH POCKETS

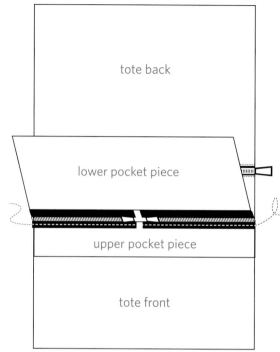

tote back

lower pocket piece

upper pocket piece

tote front

If you have a strong pattern like the fabulous houndstooth shown here, watch the pattern matching on the pocket piece. You'll want the rows to line up left to right so the pattern doesn't jump the tracks visually and make your bag look less-than-professional.

MAKE GUSSETS

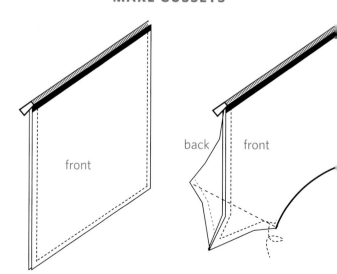

front

back   front

① **TOP ZIPPER** On the front and the back tote pieces, fold down the top edge ½" (1.3 cm) and press. Position the 16" (40.6 cm) zipper along the folded edge of the tote front so the folded fabric edge is about ⅛" (3 mm) from the zipper teeth. Use a zipper foot on your sewing machine to top stitch the zipper in place. Position tote back so the folded edge is ⅛" (3 mm) from the opposite side of the zipper. Pin (or baste) and stitch.

② **ZIPPERED POCKET** Fold down ½" (1.3 cm) on the long edge of lower and upper pocket. On the lower pocket, position the two short zippers so the opening ends are toward the center and the top tabs of the zippers just touch in the center as shown. Pin the zippers so the fabric's folded edge is about ⅛" (3 mm) from the teeth. Topstitch in place. Repeat to position and sew lower pocket on opposite side of zipper.

③ **ATTACH POCKET** Lay the tote front piece right side up. Measure 10" (25.4 cm) up from the bottom. Mark. Lay the pocket piece, with short upper pocket piece down, right sides together, with the zippers sitting on an imaginary line 10" (25.4 cm) from the bottom of the tote's front piece and the sides lining up with the sides of the main tote bag piece. Pin. Sew along the bottom stitch line on the zipper to attach the pocket to the tote (see dotted line above).

Fold the larger pocket piece down so it is parallel with the bottom edge of the tote front, lined up the sides of the pocket, and pin to secure. Pin and stitch down one side, along the bottom, and up the other side.

④ **SEW SIDE SEAMS** Fold the tote in half with the long zipper at the top and the right sides together. Align the bottom and the sides. Pin and then stitch together along the side, the bottom, and up the other side.

⑤ **BOTTOM GUSSETS** With the tote bag still inside out, grab the front piece in one hand near the bottom corner. With the other hand, grab the tote back in about the same place and pull them apart from each other so the seams line up and the point goes in the opposite direction. Measure 2½" (6.4 cm) down from the peak of the fabric point, along the center

seam line, then sew straight across horizontally (along the dotted line above) to make the gusset. Repeat on the other bottom edge of the bag. You can cut off this extra fabric if you like, though I prefer to leave it as it gives the bottom of the tote some extra padding and heft. Turn the bag right side out.

The gussets square off the bottom of the tote so it can stand up, giving the tote bag its natty shape.

(6) **ADD HANDLES** Cut a small square of firm material (you could use the bag fabric, or a piece of interfaced lining fabric) to reinforce the stitching on your handles and en-

sure that the handle has a lot to "bite." Position and pin the fabric in place on the wrong side of the fabric where you want the handles to attach. With a double strand of thread in a stout sewing needle, stitch along the pre-punched holes in your tote's handle. Tie off the thread with a sturdy knot. Repeat on each end of both handles.

(7) **LINING** Position the fusible interfacing on the wrong side of the front and back lining pieces, aligning the sides and the bottom edge. The interfacing will be about ½" (1.3 cm) short at the top to make the fold-over less bulky. Fuse the interfacing to the lining fabric following manufacturer's instructions. Pin and sew the front and back of the tote lining together as you did with the main tote. Turn the corner to create gussets as in Step 5. Fold down the top edge of the lining ½" (1.3 cm), and press.

(8) **ATTACH LINING** Stuff the lining inside the tote bag so that the wrong sides are together. With a needle and thread, and a thimble, blind stitch the lining to the zipper tab about ⅛" (3 mm) from the zipper teeth as shown. Sew all around the top edge of the bag to secure lining in place.

blind stitch

(9) **ZIPPER PULL TABS** Cut a piece of grosgrain ribbon 6" (15.2 cm) long, fold in half, then fold each end up ½" (1.3 cm) as shown, crease and pin. Sew the folded ribbon across the bottom, tight to the edge. Then sew up the center of the ribbon to about ½" (1.3 cm) below the folded edge. Open the jump ring with needle-nose pliers, and insert it through the loop at the top of the ribbon tab. Attach the jump ring to the metal zipper pull. Squeeze it tight with the pliers. Make and attach one pull for each of the three zippers.

Down-to-business LUNCH BAG

Add some color to your brown-bagging. These simple-yet-sprightly lunch sacks are made of brightly patterned, water-resistant outdoor fabric. Easy-to-clean, easy-to-sew, they make charming lunch companions.

EASY HARD
gauge of
difficulty

Bag is 10" high (plus handle), 7" wide, and 5" deep (25.4 x 17.8 x 12.7 cm)

MATERIALS

outdoor upholstery fabric

  ½ yard (45.7 cm) of lining

  ¼ yard (22.9 cm) for sides

  ¼ yard (22.9 cm) for front/back

  ¼ yard (22.9 cm) (or scrap) for flap

1 yard (91.4 cm) of colored fold-over elastic

less than ½ yard (45.7 cm) of natural 1-inch (2.5 cm) webbing in cotton, linen, or hemp

1 or 2 buttons

TOOLS

sewing kit (see page 15)

seam ripper

iron

hand-sewing needle

MEASURE & CUT

front/back (cut one)
24" (61 cm)

8" (20.3 cm)

flap (cut one)
6.5" (16.5 cm)

8" (20.3 cm)

sides (cut one)
26" (66 cm)

5.5" (14 cm)

front/back lining (cut one)
29.5" (74.9 cm)

8" (20.3 cm)

sides lining (cut one)
26" (66 cm)

5.5" (14 cm)

ASSEMBLE BAG

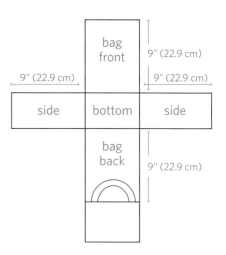

These lunch bags are fun to make because there are so many creative ways to customize them. Play with different pattern and color combinations for the front, sides, and flap. Try using a bright piece of elastic and characterful buttons for either the double-side loop or the center button closure.

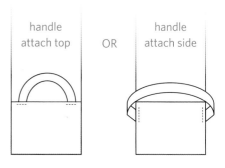

Attach top handle as per instructions in Step 1 OR attach handle on the sides by topstiching the ends to the underside of the flap in Step 8 of the process.

1 FLAP AND HANDLE

Cut about 9" (22.9 cm) of the webbing. Pin the handle ends even with the top edge of the right side of the flap, and about 1" (2.5 cm) in from the sides. With right sides together, and the handle arcing downward, pin the flap to the back panel. Sew.

2 LINE THE PANELS

With right sides together, pin the front/back panel to its lining panel, and sew around the perimeter leaving about 3" (7.6 cm) open along the side in order to turn the panel right side out. Repeat with the side panel and lining. Turn the panels through the holes so they are right side out. Pin the hole closed (you will sew it closed as part of the next Step). Press the two pieces with an iron so corners are sharp and the seams lie flat.

3 ASSEMBLE BAG

Lay the side panel face down horizontally. Lay the front/back panel down vertically on top of it to make a cross where the two arms stick out 9" (22.9 cm) and the bottom leg of the cross is also 9" (22.9 cm) long. Make sure the pieces are perpendicular to one another. Pin the pieces together. Topstitch along the edges where the two pieces overlap. This will become the bottom of the lunch bag.

4 SIDE SEAMS

Bring up the side panel and the front/back panel at the corner. The lining/wrong sides of the fabric will be together, and you will be sewing an exposed seam that shows to the outside. Lay the side panel edge along the back panel edge making sure they line up and meet at the corners as shown above. (Note how the bottom is folded diagonally to make this happen). Sew together about ¼" (6 mm) from the edge. Repeat on all four sides.

5 TOP STITCH

Add topstitching to the front flap along the sides and top about ¼" (6 mm) in from the edge. Add some extra lines of stitching along the top edge of the flap as both decoration and also to make it sturdier for the button closure. The lines of stitching shown here are about ¼" (6 mm) apart.

6 MAKE LOOP

You can use the fold-over elastic flat for this, or you can make a hipper, fancier loop by folding the elastic piece in half along its center line, and using a zigzag stitch to sew it closed. Be sure to tug gently but firmly on the elastic as you sew so the stitching won't break once its gets stretched doing its job. You will need two pieces 5½" to 6" (14 to 15.2 cm) long for the side loops (shown in Step 7), or a piece about 3½" (8.9 mm) for the center loop version (Step 8).

7 ATTACH CLOSURE

To create a bag with a two-button side closure, sew the buttons at the bottom corners of flap about 1" (2.5 cm) in from the edges. Use a seam ripper to open a ½" (1.3 cm) space in the side back seam about 4" (10.2 cm) down from the flap. Insert a loop of elastic about 5" to 6" (12.7 to 15.2 cm) long, pin in place, then sew to close. Repeat for other side.

8 ALTERNATE CLOSURE

For the center closing bag, attach a single button on the center of the flap. Center a short length of elastic on the front panel about 3" (7.6 cm) down from the top. You want the flap to cover the stitches used to attach the elastic leaving an inch or two of elastic showing below the flap edge. Sew the elastic in place, loop down, with a short horizontal run of stitches.

Farmhouse DISH TOWELS

Hunt down this scrunchy waffle-weave fabric in the utility section of any big-box fabric store. It may look nondescript on the bolt, but give it a pre-wash and the weave "blooms" into this absorbent, charming vintage look.

EASY HARD
gauge of difficulty

Makes 2 towels, 16" x 25" (40.6 x 63.5 cm)

MATERIALS

1 yard (91.4 cm) waffle-weave cotton utility cloth

1 ½ (1.4 m) yards narrow (¼ or ⅛-inch) (6 or 3 mm) satin ribbon for each towel

1 yard (91.4 cm) of embroidered ribbon or printed cotton twill tape for each towel

½ yard (45.7 cm) of 100% cotton calico print

TOOLS

sewing kit (see page 15)

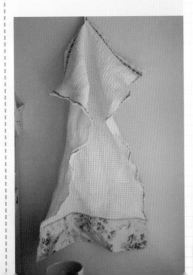

MEASURE & CUT

towel (cut two)
22" (55.9 cm)

16" (40.6 cm)

✂ cut from waffle toweling

border (cut two)
8" (20.3 cm)

17" (43.2 cm)

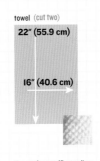

✂ cut from cotton print

Pre-wash the fabric as it shrinks pretty dramatically. But, more importantly, pre-washing serves to soften and fluff the weave. Once washed and machine dried, you can cut 2 towels out of the waffle weave purchased. Cut the fabric in half the long way and leave the finished selvage edge at the top of the towels. The weave itself serves as the perfect built-in grid to help when you are cutting the fabric and aligning the ribbon details.

① ADD THE RIBBON Use the waffle weave as your guide to pin the skinny ribbon about ½" (1.3 cm) in from the edge along the two sides of the towel. Run the ribbon in the "trough" of the waffle weave, then sew down the middle of the ribbon. Repeat on the other side.

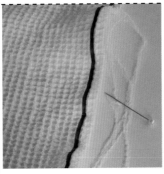

② FRAY THE EDGES Use a straight pin to tease away a loose thread from the cut edge of the waffle fabric beyond the ribbon on the sides. Tease out one thread and pull it off all the way along the edge. Continue pulling off threads until you have a nicely frayed edge—3 or 4 threads should do it. Repeat on the other side of the towel.

③ ADD THE BORDER With right sides together, pin the cotton calico border onto the bottom edge of the towel (the edge opposite the selvage edge). The border fabric will extend beyond the edge of the toweling by about ½" (1.3 cm) on each side. Sew.

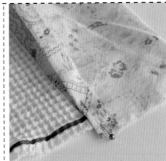

④ BORDER SIDE SEAMS Turn down the edge of the border fabric about ½" (1.3 cm), then bring this turned edge up to meet the seam sewn in Step 3. Pin the side seam and sew. Repeat on the opposite side. Now turn the fabric so the border is right side out. Make sure the turned edge pulls up and covers the raw edges. Pin. Use a tight zig-zag stitch, to sew the open border edge closed.

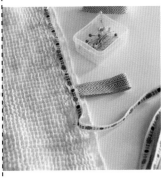

⑤ ADD RIBBON & LOOP There are two ways to add the ribbon and a hanging loop. Shown above is a two piece version that requires cutting a piece of embroidered or printed ribbon that is about 3" (7.6 cm) longer than the width of the towel. In addition, cut a piece of contrasting ribbon or twill tape for the loop that is about 5" (12.7 cm) long.

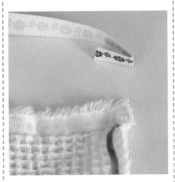

Alternatively, you can do a self-loop that requires cutting the embroidered ribbon 9" (22.9 cm) longer than the towel width.
For either version, fold the end of the embroidered ribbon over about ½" (1.3 cm).

Wrap 1" (2.5 cm) of this folded ribbon around the back of the towel and pin in place. Continue pinning the embroidered ribbon along the front top edge of the towel. If you are doing the contrasting loop, fold the contrasting ribbon in half and tuck the ends under the embroidered ribbon at the center of the towel. Pin in place so the ends are covered by the embroidered ribbon. Continue pinning, until you reach the other side of the towel and wrap the folded ribbon end around the towel as before.

For the self-loop, start by wrapping the folded ribbon ends around the back of the towel as described earlier. Pin these finished ends in place on both sides of the towel, then, working from each side toward the center, pin the embroidered ribbon in place. You will have a few inches of leftover embroidered ribbon at the center which will become your loop. For either version, machine stitch the ribbon into place along the top and bottom close to the edges of the embroidered ribbon.

Square Deal POTHOLDER

Sprinkle a dash of color into your kitchen with these handsome, helpful potholders made from wool scraps quick-felted in the washer. They're easy-to-make and easy-to-love, cook one up for your favorite chef.

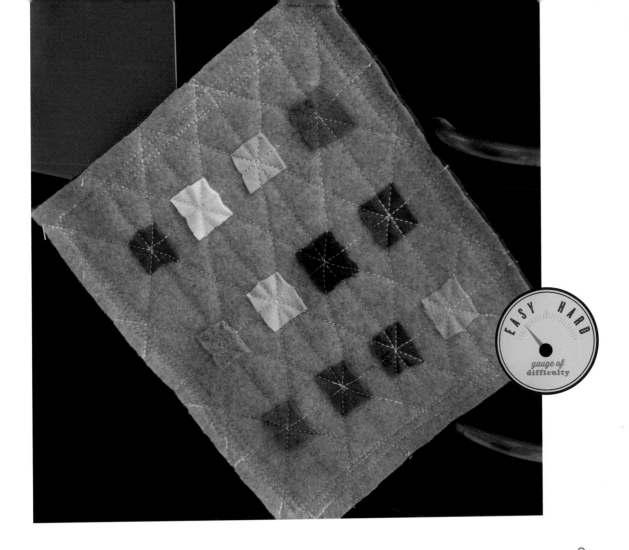

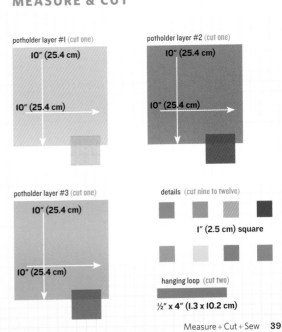

Finished potholder is about 8 ½ x 8 ½" (21.6 x 21.6 cm)

MATERIALS

the wool fabric used here should be "felted", i.e. washed and dried in a hot dryer to tighten and plump the weave. Felted sweater fabric can also be used here to great effect.

3 thick wool fabric scraps about 10" x 10" (25.4 x 25.4 cm) (they can all be one color or 3 different colors)

up to 12 small scraps of wool fabric or felt of varying colors to use for the details and hanging loop

contrasting thread

TOOLS

sewing kit *(see page 15)*

MEASURE & CUT

potholder layer #1 (cut one)

10" (25.4 cm)

10" (25.4 cm)

potholder layer #2 (cut one)

10" (25.4 cm)

10" (25.4 cm)

potholder layer #3 (cut one)

10" (25.4 cm)

10" (25.4 cm)

details (cut nine to twelve)

1" (2.5 cm) square

hanging loop (cut two)

½" x 4" (1.3 x 10.2 cm)

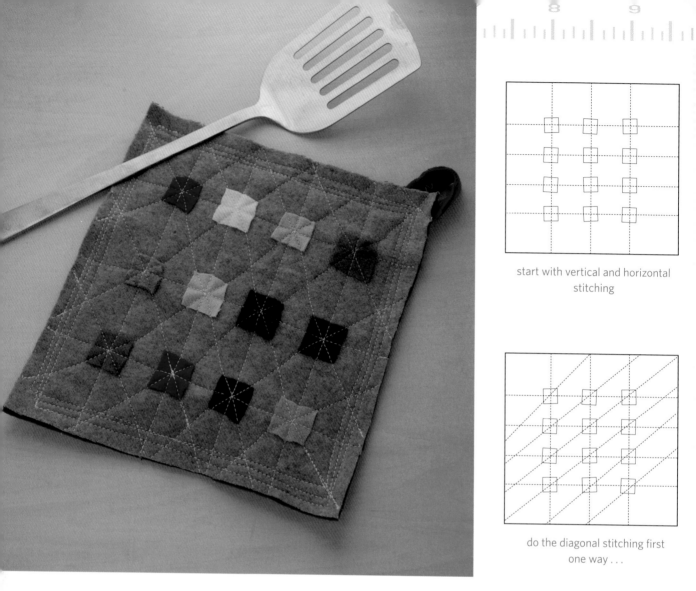

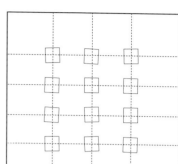

start with vertical and horizontal stitching

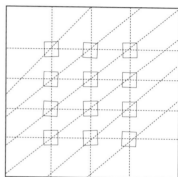

do the diagonal stitching first one way . . .

This potholder sports a grid of 3 squares across and 4 down. The horizontal space between the squares is a little greater than the vertical space. You can use a more perfectly-spaced grid of 3 squares by 3 squares if you like, but this isn't an exact science. Even the diagonal stitching doesn't mind if it is a tad wavy and meandering and approximate just so long as it finds its way through the center of each square. This potholder doesn't need geometric exactitude to be good.

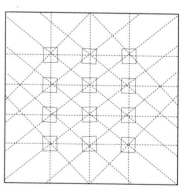

. . . then the other.

SEW THE POTHOLDER

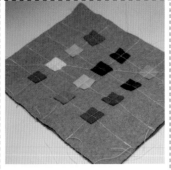

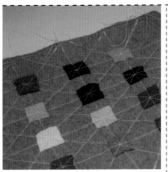

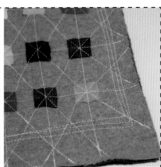

① ADD DETAILS

Stack the three layers of wool fabric on top of each other to make the potholder body. Pin. Cut 12 tiny 1" (2.5 cm) squares of wool in a variety of colors. Position them in a regular grid on the top layer. Leave a couple inches free around the perimeter. Pin the squares in place through all the layers of the potholder.

② SEW SQUARES

Start by sewing in rows and columns up through and then across the grid. Sew in a line through the center of each square vertically then horizontally.

③ SEW THE DIAGONALS

Sew diagonally through the squares starting at one end of the potholder and going to the other end. This need not be an exact science, just try to sew through the center of each square as you sew the diagonal lines. Don't worry if the lines aren't perfectly straight or exactly parallel to one another, your finished product will still be great!

④ STITCH PERIMETER

Sew a round of stitching about ¾" (1.9 cm) from the edge of your grid of little squares. Add another round of perimeter stitching about an ⅛" to a ¼" (3 to 8 mm) from the first one. No need to be to careful here, if the stitching lines undulate a little, it will give the final product more character.

⑤ TRIM TO SIZE

Cut around the outside edge of the potholder to within ¼ to ½" (.6 to 1.3 cm) of the outside round of stitching. Nice clean cuts will do the best job of showing off your three colorful layers.

⑥ MAKE LOOP

Lay the 2 loop pieces one atop the other and use a machine zig-zag stitch to sew them together down the middle. Fold the piece into a loop. Pin the two ends side-by-side in the corner of potholder. Stitch the loop into place on the back side of the potholder, then backtrack over the stitching again to hold it tight.

Save-the-date APRON

Printed linen calendars were a mid-century kitchen must-have. But now, the graphic numbers are retro-hip again. The images can be a bit dated, but with a clever twist this calendar makes a café apron whose time has come.

EASY · HARD
gauge of difficulty

Size: This is a small café apron that is about 15″ x 16″, (38.1 x 40.6 cm) for a larger apron, use two printed calendars.

MATERIALS

1 or 2 vintage calendar kitchen towels (typical size, 15–18″ [38.1–45.7 cm] wide by about 27″ [68.6 cm] long)

⅓ yard (30.5 cm) of light to medium-weight natural linen fabric for the waistband

TOOLS

sewing kit (see page 15)

MEASURE & CUT

front sides (cut two)

6″ (15.2 cm)

52″ (132.1 cm)

✂ cut from linen

If you are using a fabric with a width narrower than 52″ (132.1 cm) or if you are making the larger apron, you will need to piece together a longer strip for the waistband. In that case, cut two pieces that are each 6″ wide by 27″ long (15.2 x 68.6 cm). For the larger apron, or if you like longer ties, cut two pieces that are 30″ (76.2 cm) long.

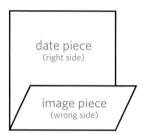

One apron makes a tidy little café apron that is big enough to cover the front of most cooks. If you would like a wider apron that offers more coverage, combine two linen kitchen calendars as shown below.

1-CALENDAR VERSION

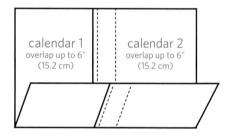

date piece
(right side)

image piece
(wrong side)

2-CALENDAR VERSION

calendar 1
overlap up to 6"
(15.2 cm)

calendar 2
overlap up to 6"
(15.2 cm)

These vintage calendar kitchen towels have a certain graphic charm, but they *also* often have truly dreadful colored illustrations printed on them. The good news? The back or wrong side of these printed illustrations are often softly colored and lightened into an abstract watercolor. This clever apron project uses the front side of the graphic date section of the calendar, then flips up the back of the illustration to make a pocket.

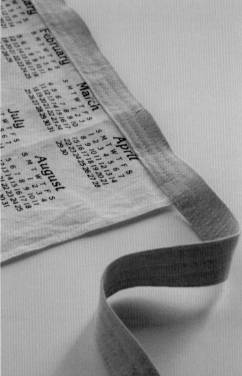

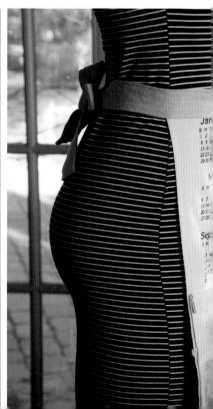

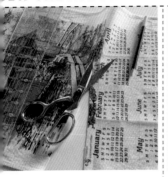

① CUT THE CALENDAR
Cut the image portion of the calendar kitchen towel from the part that has the dates.

② REASSEMBLE
Turn the image panel around so it is now at the bottom of the right-reading date portion. Pin the finished edge of the date panel (what used to be the bottom edge of the towel) over the cut edge of the image portion, overlapping about ½" (1.3 cm). Sew one row of stitching ⅛" (3 mm) in from the finished edge, then another row of stitching ¼" (6 mm) further in to secure.

③ MAKE POCKET Fold the bottom edge of image portion up about 6" to 7" (15.2 to 17.8 cm) to make the pocket. Sew along both sides of the apron about ¼" (6 mm) in from the edge to secure the corners of the pocket.

④ POCKET PARTITION
Add vertical lines of stitching that run the height of the pocket to reinforce and divide the pocket into useful sections. Sew two vertical rows of stitching about ¼" (6 mm) apart along the center line. Add more vertical lines as per your preference.

pocket sections

⑤ THE WAISTBAND
With right sides together, and the center aligned, pin then sew the waistband to the apron top. For the pieced waistband described in the **Measure & Cut** section, sew the two smaller sections together to make one longer one and align this seam with the center of the apron top. Once you have sewn the waistband section to the apron, press the bottom seam allowance up ½" (1.3 cm) with an iron all the way to the ends of the waistband ties.

⑥ FOLD THE WAISTBAND
Fold the cut edge of the waistband down so it meets the edge of the seam sewn in the last Step. Then fold this newly-folded edge down again to just cover the stitching on that seam. Pin. Work along the width of the apron. Once you get beyond the edge of the apron fabric where the waistband becomes the ties, continue folding the waistband piece down so it meets the upturned edge from the last Step. Pin.

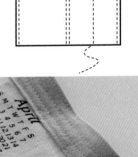

⑦ FINISH THE ENDS
Fold the end of the tie in about ½" (1.3 cm) so it folds *under* the big fold at the top of the waistband ties and the smaller folded piece at the bottom. Then pin the end closed. Sew a line of stitches about ¼" (6 mm) from the edge to close the ends and the bottom edge of the ties. Continue this stitching across the apron and to the opposite tie to finish it.

⑧ ADD REINFORCEMENT.
Add three or four rows of evenly spaced stitching the length of the waistband/ties as shown. This makes a waistband that lies flat and ties that are neater and more substantial. Plus, c'mon, it looks cool.

Tea Trivet MUG MATS

A clever bit of graphic color-blocking and modern peek-a-boo add visual octane to your tea time or coffee break.

Make a colorful stack to have around, they'll keep things tidy while they're keeping things interesting.

EASY HARD
gauge of difficulty

Makes 3 coasters, 6″ x 6″ (15.2 x 15.2 cm)

MATERIALS

¼ yard (22.9 cm) wool or wool-blend felt in charcoal

¼ yard (22.9 cm) or a 12″ (30.5 cm) square (or even less) of wool or wool-blend felt in each of three different colors

white thread

spray-on stain guard and water-proofing for fabric

¼ yard (22.9 cm) or a 12″ (30.5 cm) square of newspaper fabric for the Coffee Coaster option

TOOLS

sewing kit (see page 15)

a mug to use as a template

MEASURE & CUT

mat interior (cut one)

7″ (17.8 cm)

3.5″ (8.9 cm)

mat interior (cut one)

7″ (17.8 cm)

3.5″ (8.9 cm)

mat interior (cut one)

7″ (17.8 cm)

3.5″ (8.9 cm)

✂ cut from colored felt

mat front and back (cut two)

7″ (17.8 cm)

7″ (17.8 cm)

✂ cut from gray felt

SEW THE MUG MATS

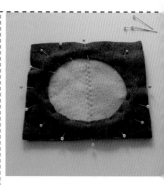

① CUT THE CIRCLE

Place your desired mug upside down on the top-layer of mat, centered. Use pencil, chalk, or marker to trace the circle. Starting in the center of the circle, snip a hole so you can get your scissors started, then cut along the marked line to remove a circle of fabric from the center.

② TWO-TONE LAYER

Place the narrow pieces for the colorful two-tone layer side-by-side on the bottom layer. Make sure the two pieces are snug together down the center line. Pin in place.

③ ZIG ZAG TOGETHER

Using a wide and loose zig-zag stitch, sew down the center between the two pieces to both sew them together and secure them to the back.

④ EDGE THE CIRCLE

Place the piece with the cutout atop the two-tone layer. Line up edges and begin pinning around the circle edge as shown. Carefully topstitch around the hole with the wide zig-zag stitch taking care that the stitches grab a bit of the circle edge and the peek-a-boo piece below.

⑤ TOP STITCH

Using your zig-zag stitch, sew around the outside edge about ½" (1.3 cm) in from the edge. Trim the felt edges to within a ¼" (6 mm) of the zig-zag stitching to straighten up the mug mat edges.
Spray with stain guard fabric treatment to keep the potholders looking fresh and stain-free.

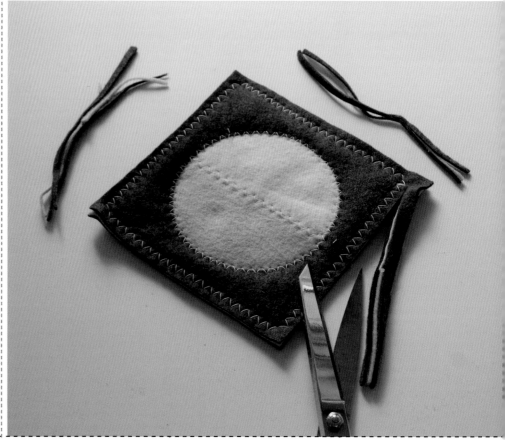

Coffee COASTER

These coasters are an ode to that classic morning combo of a newspaper and a cup of coffee. Newsprint-inspired fabric pairs with cozy felt to make these a hot spot for your morning cuppa.

and
and are
interjected
rrative
his own
ded a picture
on a donkey
retraced

Greene was sup
the capstone of
30-year underta
hould build on th

to a long list
have helped,
The list includ

few subtle
are and th
a m

MEASURE & CUT

mat layer #1 (cut one)

7" (17.8 cm)

7" (17.8 cm)

mat layer #2 (cut one)

7" (17.8 cm)

7" (17.8 cm)

✂ cut from wool felt

mat layer #4 (cut one)

7" (17.8 cm)

7" (17.8 cm)

mat layer #3 (cut one)

7" (17.8 cm)

7" (17.8 cm)

✂ cut from newspaper fabric

For material and tool information, see page 47.

(1) CUTOUT

Stack two layers of wool felt and secure with a couple of pins. Use an inverted mug as a template to trace a circle in the center of the felt. Pin around the outside edge of the circle with one or two pins as well as in the center to keep the layers aligned. Snip with scissors in the center of the circle to get the cut started, then cut around the traced line to carefully remove the center circle.

(2) ADD THE LAYERS

Add the newspaper fabric to the stack beneath the cutout you just made, then one more layer of colored felt for the bottom. Pin carefully around the cutout to secure all four layers together.

(3) TOP STITCH

Use a wide and loose zig-zag to sew around the perimeter of the circle, being sure to straddle the circle's edge to catch both the felt and the cotton fabric below.

(4) FINISH THE EDGE

Using the same wide and loose zig-zag, sew around the outside of the coaster about ½" (1.3 cm) in from the edge. Then trim the excess fabric along the outside edge to within ¼" (6 mm) of the stitching. A nice, sharp cut will really show off the colorful layers. Spray with fabric treatment to keep stains at bay.

Geometric DOPP KIT

There's a little bit of magic in these jaunty toiletry bags, and it's not a fancy toothbrush or an expensive cream.

The magic happens when the flat fabric squares pop-up to become charming, 3-dimensional travel companions.

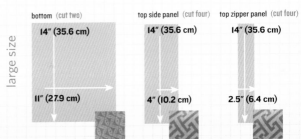

Small kit is 7" wide x 7" long x 3½" high (17.8 x 17.8 x 8.9 cm); Large kit is 7" x 10" x 3½" (17.8 x 25.4 x 8.9 cm).

MATERIALS

For small dopp kit

two ½ yard (45.7 cm) pieces of outdoor fabric in different-yet-related colors/patterns

½ yard (45.7 cm) iron-on fusible adhesive

9-inch (22.9 cm), non-separating, heavy-duty plastic zipper

½ yard (45.7 cm) of natural 1-inch (2.5 cm) wide cotton webbing

small length of ribbon for zipper pull

TOOLS

sewing kit (see page 15)

iron

zipper foot (for sewing machine)

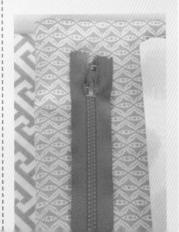

MEASURE & CUT

small size

bottom (cut two)	top side panel (cut four)	top zipper panel (cut four)
11" (27.9 cm)	11" (27.9 cm)	11" (27.9 cm)
11" (27.9 cm)	4" (10.2 cm)	2.5" (6.4 cm)

Additionally, cut all pieces out of fusible adhesive (cut one of each piece)

large size

bottom (cut two)	top side panel (cut four)	top zipper panel (cut four)
14" (35.6 cm)	14" (35.6 cm)	14" (35.6 cm)
11" (27.9 cm)	4" (10.2 cm)	2.5" (6.4 cm)

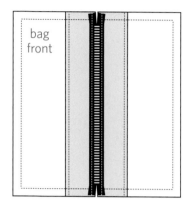

ASSEMBLE BAG

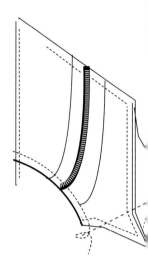

bag front

There is a little magical moment in the making of this dopp kit when it goes from flat and boring to charmingly—*and* usefully—three dimensional. Grab the flat sides of the sewn piece and pull apart in opposite directions to flare out the gusset. Then sew perpendicular to the original corner direction and this makes the vertical seam that gives the kit its height.

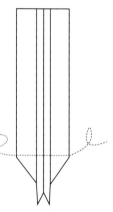

① FUSE THE FABRIC

Use fusible adhesive to fuse the two layers of fabric together. This makes each piece for this project double thick, pleasantly stiff, and more finished-looking on the inside. Put the adhesive between the wrong sides of the fabric and follow manufacturer's instructions to create a properly fused, double-sided fabric. Repeat process for all project pieces.

② ADD ZIPPER

Fold down ½" (1.3 cm) on one edge of each of the two zipper panel pieces. Press. Position the folded edge along the zipper tape with the fabric edge about ⅛" (3 mm) away from the zipped teeth. Pin to secure. Repeat on the opposite side of the zipper as shown.

③ SEW ZIPPER

Using the zipper foot for your machine, sew two lines of stitching along the zipper, with one line being about ⅛" (3 mm) from the fabric edge and the other line about ¼" (6 mm) away. Its easiest to sew on the right side of the fabric, but here is what it looks like on the wrong side.

④ ADD TAB

Add a loop of twill tape for the hanging tab on one end of the kit. Cut 4" (10.2 cm) of twill tape, fold in half, and position along the edge of the kit's bottom piece, on the right side of the fabric. The loop end should point down, away from the edge, as shown.

⑤ FINISH TOP PIECE

Sew the two side pieces to either side of the zipper panel pieces to complete the top piece. Then, with right sides together, stack the top piece, with the zipper part-way open, atop the bottom piece, lining up edges. Pin, then sew all the way around the perimeter. Note the red dot on the photo above. It is the point at which you will grab the fabric in order to turn the corner and make the gusset in the next Step.

⑥ MAKE GUSSETS

Grab the fabric at the red-dot point on both the front and the back side of the assembled piece. Pull apart

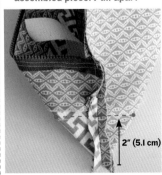

2" (5.1 cm)

and the corner will turn with the tip pointing in the opposite direction. Pin the corners. Insert the end of a 7" (17.8 cm) piece of twill tape into the new corner point. Pin to secure. Measure down from the corner tip 2" (5.1 cm) and mark a horizontal line (see photo at left). Sew along this line and then trim the corner as shown above. Repeat on the other corner of the kit inserting the opposite end of the twill tape into *this* gusset to create the kit's handle.

⑦ TURN THE BAG

Turn the bag using the zipper opening so the right side is out. Note how the handle looks neat and sharp with its ends tucked into the gussets. To make the zipper easier to open and close, loop a 6" to 8" (15.2 to 20.3 cm) piece of skinny grosgrain ribbon through the hole in the zipper pull, knot tight, and trim the ends.

Fold 'n' Go SHOE ROLL

Here's the nattiest way to pack your favorite sneakers, bucks, or loafers on your next adventure. This elegantly simple design positions shoes toe-to-heel so they are compact yet perfectly, protected.

Folded size about 16" x 8" (40.6 x 20.3 cm), each shoe compartment is about 15" x 7" (38.1 x 17.8 cm) (which is ample for most men's and women's average shoes)

MATERIALS

½ to ¾ yard (45.7 to 68.6 cm) of 54-inch wide medium to heavyweight fabric like ticking, cotton duck, denim, twill, or barkcloth

¼ yard (22.9 cm) of cotton canvas

2 buttons

½ yard (45.7 cm) of ½-inch (1.3 cm) wide black elastic

optional: scrap of natural cotton canvas for the monogram

optional: ink/ink pad for cloth

TOOLS

sewing kit (see page 15)

optional: alphabet rubber stamps or stencils

MEASURE & CUT

front sides (cut one)

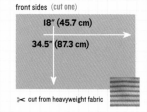

18" (45.7 cm)

34.5" (87.3 cm)

✂ cut from heavyweight fabric

front sides (cut one)

10" (25.4 cm)

*18" (45.7 cm)

✂ cut from canvas

✱ This has purposely been cut a little longer than needed so you can adjust it to fit perfectly in its place in Step 3

ASSEMBLE THE SHOE ROLL

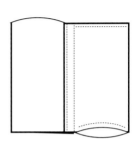

folds
fold in each so there
is about a ¼" (6 mm)
overlap on each side in the
middle.

seams
sew the center seams
about ¼" (6 mm) inch in
from each edge. Sew the
bottom edge closed to
make the shoe pocket on
the left side, and the top
edge closed on the right.

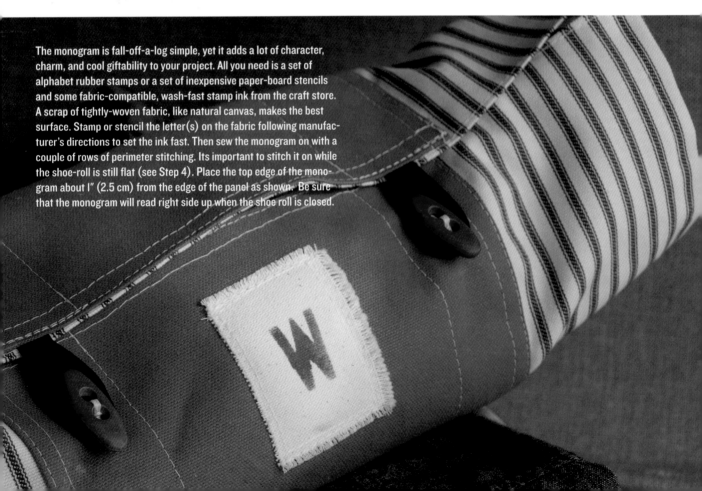

The monogram is fall-off-a-log simple, yet it adds a lot of character, charm, and cool giftability to your project. All you need is a set of alphabet rubber stamps or a set of inexpensive paper-board stencils and some fabric-compatible, wash-fast stamp ink from the craft store. A scrap of tightly-woven fabric, like natural canvas, makes the best surface. Stamp or stencil the letter(s) on the fabric following manufacturer's directions to set the ink fast. Then sew the monogram on with a couple of rows of perimeter stitching. Its important to stitch it on while the shoe-roll is still flat (see Step 4). Place the top edge of the monogram about 1" (2.5 cm) from the edge of the panel as shown. Be sure that the monogram will read right side up when the shoe roll is closed.

1 HEM THE EDGES

Starting with the long sides of the main rectangle, fold the edges over ½" (1.3 cm) and then roll that fold ½" (1.3 cm) more. Pin and sew about ⅜" (9.5 mm) in from the fold. Do the same thing on the short side of the rectangle until the entire piece sports a neat, finished edge.

2 THE BASIC STRUCTURE

Make the folds that will eventually define the shoe pockets: Lay the rectangle face down and fold up first one short edge and then the other toward the center. Find the point where the two edges overlap one another by 1¼" (3.2 cm). Pin the overlap. Now center those overlapping edges in the middle of the overall piece as though they are the spine of a book. Smooth out the folded square and pin along the edges (outlined above in red). Sew ¼" (6 mm) in from these folded edges.

3 MAKE THE PANEL

Fold the edge along the long side down ½" (1.3 cm), pin, then sew about ⅜" (9.5 mm) in from the edge. This panel wants a custom fit between the two rows of stitching you made in Step 2. Fold one short side down ½" (1.3 cm) and pin, but then try the canvas panel on the folded piece from Step 2 to make sure it fits edge-to-edge. You might need to cut a little off the unfinished end and *then* fold it down ½" (1.3 cm), pin, and sew both ends as before.

4 AFFIX THE PANEL

Open the large rectangle flat and position the panel between the two rows of stitching centered top to bottom. Pin in place. Stitch around the perimeter. On one of the short ends, leave 1" (2.5 cm) on each end of the panel open. This is where the elastic will go in Step 7. Then sew two horizontal lines of stitching about 1¾" (4.4 cm) from the long edge of the panel (for decoration). *Now* is the time to attach the optional monogram. (see opposite page)

5 CENTER SEAM

Flip the piece over and fold in the left flap. Pin then sew the length of the center line ⅛" (3 mm) in from the edge, then a second row of stitching at ⅜" (9.5 mm) in. Now fold over the flap on the right hand side, pin and sew 2 rows of stitching along its edge to make the center "spine" as shown below.

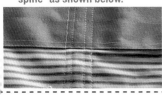

6 FINISH THE SHOE POCKETS.

The most efficient way to pack shoes is nested together toe to heel. To encourage that configuration, sew the left hand shoe pocket closed at the bottom, and the right hand pocket closed at the top. Sew the pocket closed all the way by stitching a row about ⅛" (3 mm) in from the edge going from the center spine to the outer edge.

7 ADD ELASTIC LOOPS

Cut pieces of elastic about 4" (10.2 cm) long and fold in half. Slip the ends of the elastic loop into the gaps left in the panel's perimeter stitching back in Step 4. (If you forgot to leave the gaps, get out your seam ripper now). Position as shown. Pin in place and sew the gap closed stitching over the elastic at least twice to secure.

8 ATTACH BUTTONS

Make sure your buttons are large enough for the elastic to get a good grip on. Use a double thread in your needle to attach them securely. The center of the buttons should be about 1¾" (4.4 cm) from the shoe-roll edge lining up directly across from the elastic loops. Be sure to *only* sew through the canvas panel and the top layer of the shoe roll so you don't sew the shoe pocket itself closed.

Pojagi-inspired SHADE

Buckram is a 100% cotton utility fabric normally used to give stiffness to things like baseball caps and books. But it makes an unexpectedly perfect light-diffusing, non-fraying fabric to make a glorious window shade.

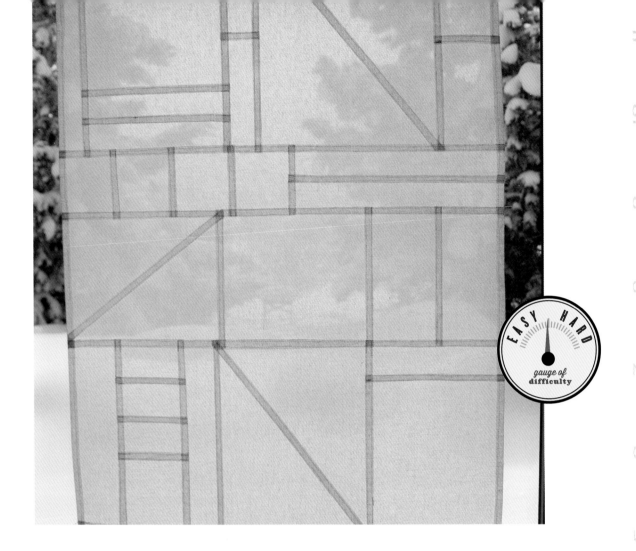

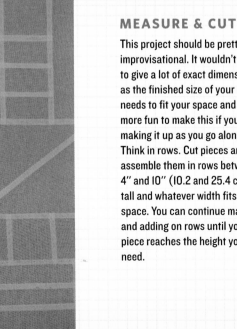

Made to measure—customize for your window size

MATERIALS

100% cotton buckram comes in 20" to 24" (50.8 to 61 cm) widths. You'll need at least a yard (91.4 cm) for even a small window. You want to be able to add as many seams as you want to make an interesting pattern so buy 1 ½ to 2 times as much as you would need to cover your window to allow for lots of cutting and seaming

dowel for hanging

TOOLS

sewing kit *(see page 15)*

optional: rotary tool and mat with metal or plastic straight-edge

MEASURE & CUT

This project should be pretty improvisational. It wouldn't help to give a lot of exact dimensions as the finished size of your shade needs to fit your space and its more fun to make this if you are making it up as you go along. Think in rows. Cut pieces and assemble them in rows between 4" and 10" (10.2 and 25.4 cm) tall and whatever width fits your space. You can continue making and adding on rows until your piece reaches the height you need.

SEW THE SHADE

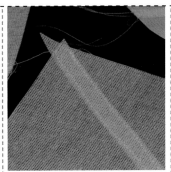
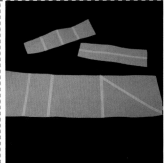

① START SIMPLE
Start with a few simple shapes like a couple of squares, a long rectangle. Start to imagine a horizontal row. Maybe you leave the square whole, but cut the second square in half. The strip could have a couple small squares cut from it. Another square could be cut on the diagonal.

② SEW PIECES TOGETHER
Buckam is wonderful because it cuts beautifully, almost like paper, and it doesn't fray at all. All you have to do for the seams is to overlap the edges of the pieces by ½" (1.3 cm), pin in a couple places, then sew.

③ DOUBLE STITCHING
The seams are neatest if you stitch two rows as close as possible to each raw edge of the overlap as seen above. This makes a solid seam that lies flat and just intensifies the graphic lines that each seam creates in the overall project.

④ START WITH A ROW
Assemble your project in horizontal bands or rows of seamed-together shapes. The rows need to be an inch or two wider than your target finished size. For example, this first band has a square cut in half and seamed onto a plain square, which was in turn seamed on to a square that is cut into two triangles and seamed on the diagonal. Be prepared to trim pieces a bit to get them to all fit into your horizontal row.

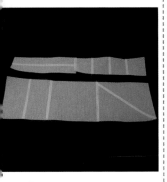

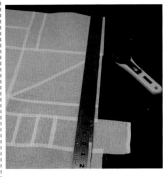
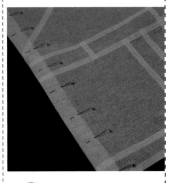

⑤ ADD MORE ROWS
The next horizontal row is made up of a skinny rectangle cut into 4 small squares seamed together. Another slightly wider rectangle is cut into long, skinny strips and pieced together horizontally. Both pieces are then seamed together to make a long narrow band. Make sure the long edges of each row are straight before proceeding. Use the straightedge and the rotary tool to trim if needed.

⑥ KEEP ADDING ROWS
As you go along, you will get more confident in piecing together shapes then seaming those shapes together into longer horizontal rows. Note that each individual piece doesn't need to be complex, one or two seams on any given piece is often enough. But once those pieces are all put together, they seem more complex, and frankly, better thought out. It really is an exciting improvisational project.

⑦ KEEP IT STRAIGHT
Its important to keep the interface between each band straight so the shade itself is straight and square. Use the straightedge and rotary tool at each juncture to square up the edge.

⑧ HEM ALL AROUND
Once your piece has enough rows to reach your desired height, simply fold the sides in ½" (1.3 cm) and sew. Buckram is so easy to fold, again, you can crease it like paper. Sew another ½" (1.3 cm) hem on the bottom, but fold the top edge down between 1 and 1½" (2.5 and 3.8 cm) to make a rod pocket for a dowel to hang the shade.

Festival **DRESS**

Pintucks are all that's needed to give this boho confection its fit and flare. Perfect for a concert, a day at the beach, even a summer night out, this dress makes up quick as a wink for the price of a song . . .

EASY HARD
gauge of difficulty

Comes in three sizes: small, medium, large
(please see instructions at right for size conversions and an explanation)

MATERIALS

2 yards (1.8 cm) very light-weight cotton like voile, lawn, gauze, etc.

3 yards (2.7 m) ½" (1.3 cm) single-fold bias tape

TOOLS

sewing kit *(see page 15)*

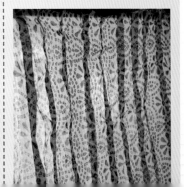

MEASURE & CUT

dress (cut one)

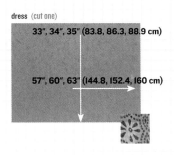

33", 34", 35" (83.8, 86.3, 88.9 cm)

57", 60", 63" (144.8, 152.4, 160 cm)

For size small (34" bust [86.4 cm]), cut piece 57" wide x 33" high (144.8 x 83.8 cm).
For size medium (37" bust [94 cm]), cut piece 60" wide x 34" high (152.2 x 86.4 cm).
For size large (40" bust [101.6 cm]), cut piece 63" wide x 35" high (160 x 88.9 cm).
Follow same instructions for size and number of pintucks in the following pages for all three sizes.

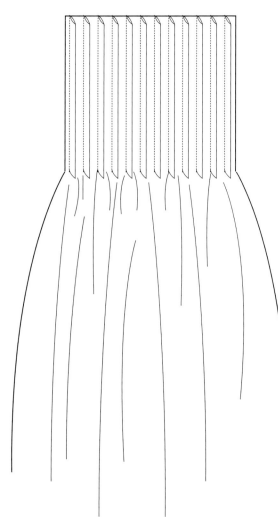

HEMMING THE DRESS

The length of the dress will depend on your height and where you like your dresses to hit—at the knee or above it. Try the dress on after you have completed all the Steps at right. Mark the spot where you would like the dress to hit, then add two inches more length for hem. Measure down from the top to your mark, use this measurement to mark your length around the dress bottom. Cut off any excess. Fold the hem up first ½" (1.3 cm) then ½" (3.8 cm). Hand sew with a hem stitch.

PINTUCKS

The pintucks on this dress are really just sewn folds. Unlike the pintucks you see in tuxedo shirts where the fold is to the outside of the garment, these pintucks have the fold and the sewn seam to the inside.

1 FIRST PINTUCK

Fold the fabric in half along the long side. Measure 12" (30.5 cm) down the fold from the top edge. Mark with a pin, pencil, or pen. Pin a seam down to that 12" (30.5 cm) mark. Sew down that length, ½" (1.3 cm) in from the fold.

2 MEASURE BETWEEN TUCKS

Position your tape measure at the bottom of the last seam line sewn in Step 1. Measure 2 ½" (6.4 cm) over from that stitching line and mark. Repeat measuring and marking the 2 ½" (6.4 cm) point at the top of that same line of stitching. Pinch the fabric at both those marks and make a fold along that line. This fold will be the next pintuck. Pin, then sew ½" (1.3 cm) in from this fold line.

3 CONTINUE PINTUCKING

Pin and sew as before 12" (30.5 cm) of seam ½" (1.3 cm) in from edge. Continue measuring, marking, and sewing the pin tucks across the entire width of fabric until you have completed 23 total pintucks, twelve on each side of the center line pintuck you started with.

4 SIDE SEAMS

Once all the pintucks are completed, fold the fabric in half, right sides together, to line up the unfinished edges to make the seam at center back. Pin. Measure down 4" (10.2 cm) from the top and mark. Stitch from the bottom edge of the dress to this marked point, and backstitch to secure. Leave the remainder of the seam to the top edge of the dress open. This will be the back opening for the dress.

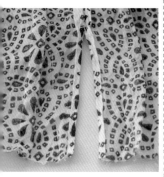

5 FINISH BACK OPENING

Fold down the edges of each side of this opening first ¼" (6 mm), then another ¼" (6 mm). Pin, then sew along the folded edges to secure and to finish this back opening. Sew a short line or two of stitching horizontally across the bottom edge of the opening to reinforce.

6 CENTER DETAIL

Find the center front pintuck. Sew two rows of long length stitches on either side of the pintuck seam running about 2" (5.1 cm) in length. Pull on the threads from the top to gather the fabric as shown. Tie to hold.

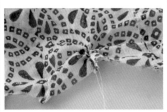

7 TRIM THE TOP

Leaving a tail of about 16" (40.6 cm), begin pinning the single-fold bias tape over the top edge of the dress so that ¼" (6 mm) of the tape folds down on both the front and the back side. Pin generously to hold. Work your way around the entire top edge and leave another tail of bias tape at the other end for a tie. Either sew this slowly, removing pins as you go, or baste first and then sew. Fold each of the tail pieces in half and sew closed to make the two ties at the back opening.

8 MAKE STRAPS

Cut two pieces of bias tape 18" (45.7 cm) long. Fold them in half along the center line, pin then sew. Position one end of the strap along the back edge (as shown) about 3" (7.6 cm) in from the back opening. Sew to secure. Try on the dress, flip the strap over your shoulder and position the other end of the strap on the top edge about 4" to 4 ½" (10.2 to 11.4 cm) from the center. Mark the comfortable length on the strap, remove the dress and sew the front strap in position. Repeat on the other strap.

Tipped Linen JACKET

A go-to city topper that puts some panache into any casual look. Deceptively simple to make, it's nothing but a small collection of rectangles that reads flirtier and more curvaceous than geometry says it ever should.

EASY HARD

gauge of difficulty

Comes in two sizes: extra small/small and medium/large
(please see page at right for size conversions)

MATERIALS

2 yards (1.8 m) light- to
medium-weight natural linen

2 packages (about 12+ feet
[3.7 + m]) of ½-inch (1.3
cm) or wider 1-inch (2.5 cm)
single-fold cotton bias tape
in black or cream

TOOLS

sewing kit *(see page 15)*

MEASURE & CUT

back (cut one)

22", 23" (55.9, 58.4 cm)

20" 21" (50.8, 53.3 cm)

sides (cut two)

22", 23" (55.9, 58.4 cm)

11", 11.5" (27.9, 29.2 cm)

sleeves (cut two)

22", 23" (55.9, 58.4 cm)

17", 17.5" (43.2, 44.5 cm)

collar (cut one)

↓ **5.5", 6"** (14, 15.2 cm)

16.5", 16.75" (41.9, 42.5 cm)

Sizing for extra small/small and medium/large

ASSEMBLE

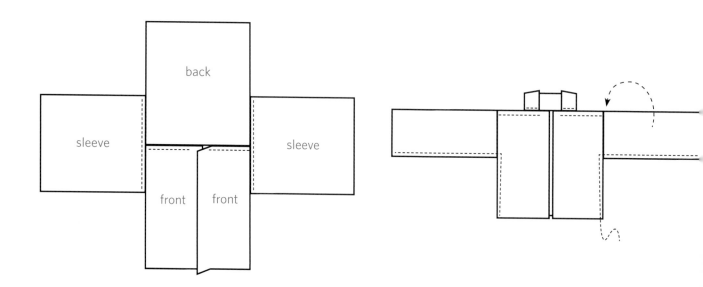

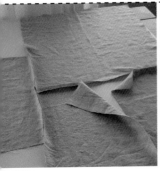

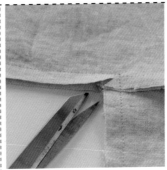

① ASSEMBLE THE PIECES

Pin the left front to the back piece, right sides together, and sew a seam that starts at the edge and goes in about 6" (15.2 cm) (for smaller size, 6 ½" [16.5 cm] for the larger). Repeat the same on the other side with the right front piece. Lay the assembled front and back face down and flat. Pin the sleeve, right sides together, along the edge of the front/back piece lining up the center of the sleeve with the shoulder seam. Pin then sew. Repeat for other sleeve.

② SIDE AND SLEEVE SEAMS

Fold the entire assembled piece in half along the shoulder seams as shown. Align the sides of the jacket and the bottom of the sleeves making sure the seams under the arm meet at the corner. Pin then sew up the side of the jacket, making a 90 degree turn at the underarm, and continuing until the sleeve end. Repeat on the other side of the jacket with the other arm.

③ CLIP THE CORNER

With the points of your scissors snip into the underarm seam about ¼" (6 mm) right at the corner. Be careful not to cut too deep and accidentally cut the thread and stitches. Repeat on other sleeve.

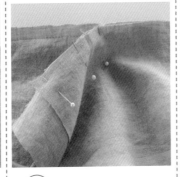

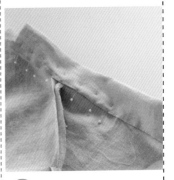

④ CENTER THE COLLAR

With right sides together, center the collar piece on the center back of the jacket. Pin the collar in place along the back pinning up to the shoulder seam on either side. Sew this length of the back collar, from shoulder seam to shoulder seam.

⑤ MAKE THE TURN

At the point where the jacket front meets the jacket back the collar makes a turn. From here to the end, it will attach to the front piece. Pin the collar to the front piece along the top edges. The end of the collar will fall a couple of inches short of the end of front piece as seen here. Sew the collar onto the front piece starting at the point where the seam from Step 5 ended. Repeat on the opposite front piece.

⑥ FOLD THE COLLAR

Fold the top edge of the collar down ½" (1.3 cm). Then fold the collar in half so the folded edge just covers the seam that attaches it to the jacket back and fronts. Pin down the collar pressing the seam allowances upward so they will be hidden inside the finished collar.

⑦ FINISH THE COLLAR

Use a needle and thread to hand sew the collar closed. Tiny, hidden stitches should do the trick. Work across the full length of the collar making sure to fully enclose the seam and seam allowances from preceding Steps. Both the front and the back of the collar will show in the finished jacket, so be sure to sew nice invisible stitches here.

SEW THE JACKET

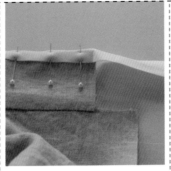

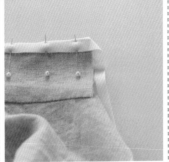

⑧ **CUT DOWN THE LAPEL**
In order for the bias tape trim to fit properly on the collar in the next Step, you have to trim away excess fabric from the top of the front "lapel." Cut the seam allowance away from the notch in the collar/lapel as shown above. If you don't trim this extra fabric away, the notch in the jacket's lapel will fall above the base of the collar, looking odd and just plain wrong. Trim so the right angle of the lapel is even with the collar's base.

⑨ **ADD BIAS TRIM**
Begin adding the bias tape at the middle of the collar back. Center the bias tape on the collar edge and then smooth it down on both the front and the back so an equal amount of bias tape falls on either side of the collar. Pin. These pictures show the wider 1" (2.5 cm) bias tape. The jacket on the model was trimmed with the narrower ½" (1.3 cm) variety. Both look natty in their own ways. The wider tape might be easier to work with for the beginning stitcher.

⑩ **TURN THE CORNER**
At the end of the collar make a 45 degree fold in the bias tape to make a neat, sharp corner. Fold the vertical piece of bias tape over the vertical portion of the collar. You will have a diagonal seam on the tape right at the corner. Along the way, make sure the tape is even and lines up on both the front and the back sides.

⑪ **ANOTHER CORNER**
Use the same technique as Step 3 to turn the inverted corner at the base of the collar. Then repeat Step 3 for the 90 degree corner at the lapel. Continue working the bias tape along the edge of the jacket down the front, across the bottom, up the other side, through all the lapel turns to the center of the collar back. Fold under the end of the bias tape and lap over the beginning of the tape from Step 2. Baste first, then sew along the tape edge to secure.

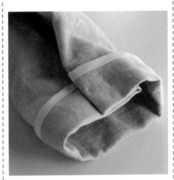

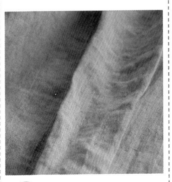

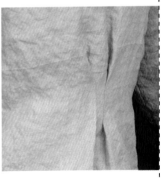

⑫ **HEM THE SLEEVE** Turn up the bottom edge of the sleeve first ½" (1.3 cm) then 3" to 3 ½" (7.6 to 8.9 cm) to make a deep cuff as shown. Sew around the upper edge of the cuff about ⅛" (3 mm) from the edge. Then add bias tape to the bottom of the cuffed edge starting at the sleeve's seam. Pin the bias tape around the sleeve bottom, then fold in and overlap the tape end as before at the seam as done in Step 4. Sew the tape to secure.

⑬ **COMPLETE THE CUFF**
To complete, fold cuff up so the bias trim is at the top edge of the cuff. Fold a 2" (5.1 cm) section of the cuff across the sleeve horizontally to make the sleeve opening tighter. Secure with a button or a few hand-sewn stitches as shown.

⑭ **SIMPLE PLEAT**
This detail will give the jacket more shape. Working from the inside of the jacket back, pinch about 1" (2.5 cm) of fabric on one side of the center back about 6" (15.2 cm) from the bottom edge. Pin this ½" (1.3 cm) seam for about 3 vertical inches (7.6 cm) up the back of the jacket. Sew. Repeat on the other side of the center back to create 2 parallel seam/pleats as shown above.

You can make the seam wider, up to a 1" (2.5 cm) seam, if you want more "pinch" at the waist. Repeat on the other side of the center back of the jacket to create the pleat detail shown above.

Summer Cloud BLOUSE

This beautiful, lightweight, sheer blouse is made perfectly discreet by strategic draping of the fabric.

Its a deceptively simple design that creates a surprisingly complex and sophisticated silhouette.

EASY HARD
gauge of difficulty

Comes in two sizes: extra small/small and medium/large
(please see page at right for size conversions)

MATERIALS

1½ yards (1.4 m) lightweight,
sheer cotton, cotton voile,
or cotton lawn, are all good
choices or a lightweight silk
or rayon could work as long
as its not too slippery

TOOLS

sewing kit *(see page 15)*

MEASURE & CUT

back (cut one)
23.5″, 24.5″ (59.7, 62.2 cm)

front (cut two)
23.5″, 24.5″ (59.7, 62.2 cm)

22″, 23″ (55.9, 58.4 cm)

19″, 19.5″ (48.3, 49.5 cm)

sleeves (cut one)
15.5″, 16″ (39.4, 40.6 cm)

**15.5″, 16″
(39.4, 40.6 cm)**

✂ cut this square in half on the diagonal

Sizing for extra small/small and medium/large

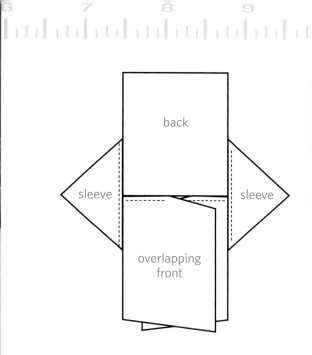

sleeve · back · sleeve · overlapping front

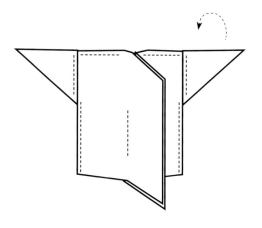

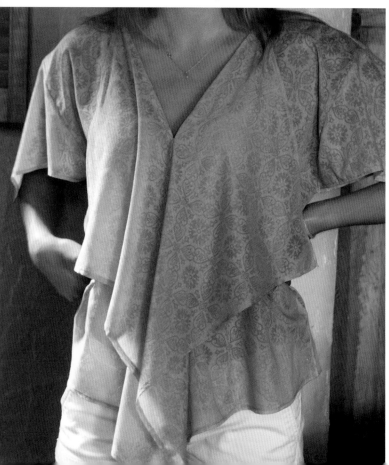

SEW THE BLOUSE

① SHOULDER SEAMS

Pin the fronts to the back of the shirt, with right sides together, lining up the outside and the top edges. The edge of the fronts that are toward the center will overlap each other by several inches. Sew shoulder seams along the top edge of each front piece. Start at the outside, and sew in 6 ¼" (15.9 cm) toward the center. Repeat on both shoulder seams.

② MAKE SLEEVES

Cut the smaller-sized square on the diagonal to make the sleeves. Be careful not to pull the fabric out of shape as you are cutting (this diagonal, or bias, grain of the fabric will have a lot of stretch). Hem along the two perpendicular edges of the sleeve, but not the diagonal one. To make a rolled hem, fold the sleeve edge ¼" (6 mm) then ¼" (6 mm) again. Pin, then sew the hem close to the edge. Repeat on the other sleeve.

③ SEW ON THE SLEEVES

Line up the center of the sleeve triangle with the shoulder seam of the front/back blouse piece. With right sides together, pin along this edge then sew a ½" (1.3 cm) seam to attach the sleeve. Again, take care not to stretch the sleeve piece along this bias edge. Repeat for the other sleeve.

④ SEW SIDE SEAMS

Fold the entire assemblage in half along the shoulder seams with right sides together. Pin along the sides starting at the bottom edge of the sleeve. Sew the side seam. Repeat on the other side of the blouse.

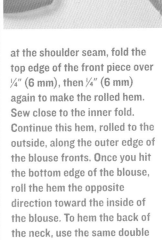

⑤ FINISH EDGES

Because the front of this blouse drapes *outward*, the finished side of the front pieces should be on what is normally considered the wrong side of the fabric. However, this wrong-side hem should *only* happen on the top of the front piece and the front's outer edge. For the back of the neck and the bottom hem of the blouse, the hem should be folded toward the inside as you would normally do. Starting

at the shoulder seam, fold the top edge of the front piece over ¼" (6 mm), then ¼" (6 mm) again to make the rolled hem. Sew close to the inner fold. Continue this hem, rolled to the outside, along the outer edge of the blouse fronts. Once you hit the bottom edge of the blouse, roll the hem the opposite direction toward the inside of the blouse. To hem the back of the neck, use the same double fold hem to turn down the seam allowance along the back edge.

⑥ FRONT SEAM

Lay the blouse on its side with *wrong* sides together. Line up the two front piece edges as shown. Measure down from the top 7" (17.8 cm) and in from the hemmed edge 7 ½" (19 cm). Place a pin to mark this spot. From this pin measure down 10" (25.4 cm) and in the same 7 ½" (19 cm) from that outer edge. Mark with a second pin. Sew a line of stitching vertically between these two pins to close the front, define the neckline, and create the pretty drape of the blouse.

⑦ NEED A PLEAT?

Try on your new blouse. If you would like a little more of a "nip" at the waist, use the technique in Step 7 of the Tipped Linen Jacket project. This easy-to-add pleat will give the blouse just a little more shape.

Four Square SKIRT

This easy, 4 panel skirt borrows the best from the classic A-line as well as the flirty flip of a kick pleat to give your own curves all the shape they could want. Make sure you choose fabric with a little bit of stretch for a smooth fit.

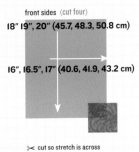

EASY — *HARD*

**gauge of
difficulty**

Comes in three sizes: small, medium, large
(please see page at right for size conversions and an explanation)

MATERIALS

1 ¼ yards (1.1 m) of
fabric with a little
stretch like a stretch
denim or twill. Look for
a fabric that has a small
percentage (3% or so)
of lycra or elastane

one large sew-on snap

TOOLS

sewing kit *(see page 15)*

MEASURE & CUT

front sides *(cut four)*

18" 19", 20" (45.7, 48.3, 50.8 cm)

16", 16.5", 17" (40.6, 41.9, 43.2 cm)

✂ cut so stretch is across
not up and down

Sizing for small, medium, and large
sizes are listed on the cutting diagram
at left. Be sure to utilize a fabric that
has a little stretch to it for a smoother,
more forgiving fit. The horizontal dimension dictates the size of the skirt,
the length can be modified based on
your height and also the length of
skirt you prefer. The dimension length
given includes allowances for 2" (5.1
cm) of hem, 1" (2.5 cm) at the top,
and 1" (2.5 cm) at the bottom of each
panel. So, the 18" (45.7 cm) length
panel will result in a 16" (40.6 cm)
long skirt. Measure from just below
your waist to the point on your leg
where you would like the skirt to fall.
Then add 2" (5.1 cm) to this length.
This is the dimension you should use
in cutting your four skirt panels.

FOUR PANEL SKIRT

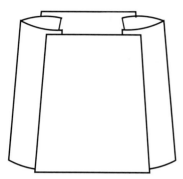

The skirt is made by 4 angled panels. The front and back panel wrap and overlap the two side pieces. In front, this overlap creates the room for pockets.

Sew the 4 panel pieces together

Complete the back panel

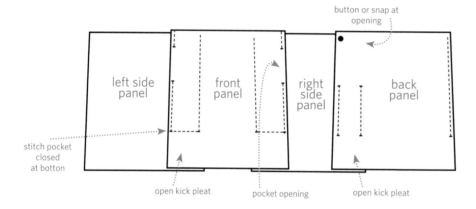

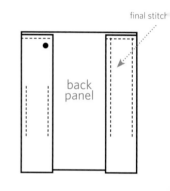

left side panel

front panel

right side panel

back panel

button or snap at opening

stitch pocket closed at bottom

open kick pleat

pocket opening

open kick pleat

back panel

final stitch

1 ANGLE THE PIECES

Fold each skirt panel in half the long way. Measure in 2" (5.1 cm) on the top edge. Mark with a pencil or just with a pin. Angle a long straight edge from the bottom corner of the folded fabric to the mark. Use a pencil to trace the angled cutting line. Cut the fabric piece (both layers) along that line to make an A-line angled piece. Repeat on all four panels.

2 FINISH THE PANEL SIDES

Fold the edge of the skirt panel over ½" (1.3 cm), then ½" (1.3 cm) again. Pin and then sew. If the fabric is a little bit thicker, go for a ⅜" (9.5 mm) fold each time and the extra thickness of the fabric will eat up the extra ⅛" (3 mm) adding up to a total of 1" (2.5 cm) used for hemming each side. Repeat on both side edges of all four panels.

3 ASSEMBLE THE SKIRT

Acquaint yourself with the drawings at left, they might give a clearer view of how the skirt comes together. Measure in 3 ¾" (9.5 cm) (from the top and bottom edge of a panel piece. Mark with pins or pencil. Lay another panel under this first one aligning its edge with the marks so that the piece overlaps the edge this same distance all the way down. The underlying panel will be your left side panel, the overlapping one is your front.

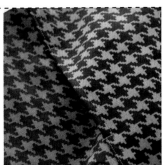

4 SEW PANELS

Where the front panel attaches to the side, sew the following: From the top edge of the skirt, sew down 2" (5.1 cm) and stop. Measure down 7" (17.8 cm), then sew from that mark another 5" (12.7 cm) to the point 14" (35.6 cm) down from the top. This leaves open the pocket and a kick pleat at the bottom of the skirt. Sew about ⅛" (3 mm) away from the edge. Add cross-stitching bar tacks at the starting/stopping points to reinforce the stitching as shown above. Repeat on the right side panel.

5 SEW INSIDE SEAMS

Along the inside edge of the overlapped panel, sew close to the edge starting at the top, and sewing down to the kick-pleat. Sew horizontally over to the bottom of the stitching from Step 4. This will close the bottom of the pocket. Repeat on the right side panel.

6 SEW BACK SEAMS

Repeat Step 3 to position overlap on panels. For the opening at the back, start the stitching 6" (15.2 cm) down from the top, then stitch down to the top of the kick-pleat as in the previous Steps. Repeat on the inside overlapped panel, starting down 6" (15.2 cm) here as well and ending at the kick-pleat. On the back seam without the opening, start stitching at the top edge of the skirt and continue down to kick-pleat height on both outer seam and inner overlap. Use bar tacks to reinforce the openings.

7 TRIM AND HEM THE PANELS

Now that all the skirt panels are sewn together, trim the bottom and the top edge of the skirt to make all the panels line up evenly. Turn down the top edge ½" (1.3 cm), then ½" (1.3 cm) again to make the waistband. Try on the skirt to check for length. Trim more off if skirt is too long, otherwise, fold up each individual panel ½" (1.3 cm), then ½" (1.3 cm) more to hem.

8 ADD A SNAP

Hand sew a large snap in place to close the opening in the skirt back. Sew the male half of the snap on the waistband close to the edge as shown. Position the female half in line with the top of the back seam stitching on the waistband. Check to make sure the opening doesn't pull or bunch when the snap is closed. Sew with doubled thread to secure.

Simple Silky T-SHIRT

Sometimes you want to throw on something simple and weightless and easy like a T-shirt but you want it sleeker, silkier, and prettier than a T. This is that shirt. Astonishingly, it's made of nothing but two squares and a button.

EASY HARD

gauge of difficulty

Comes in three sizes: small, medium, large
(please see page at right for size conversions)

MATERIALS

1¼ yards (1.1 m) lightweight
cotton sateen, cotton lawn,
lightweight silk, or rayon

one beautiful big button

TOOLS

sewing kit *(see page 15)*

MEASURE & CUT

Front and Back (cut two)

26", 27", 28" (66, 68.6, 71.1 cm)

22", 23",24.5" (55.9, 58.4, 62.2 cm)

Sizing for small,
medium,
large

ASSEMBLE

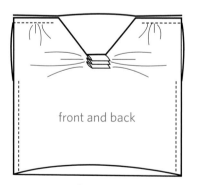

front and back

front and back

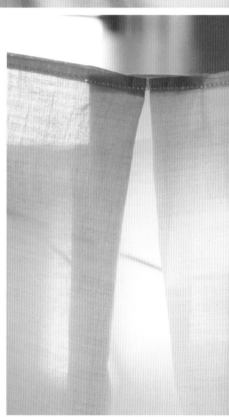

SEW THE SHIRT

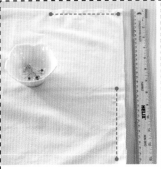

① **SEW FRONT TO BACK**
With right sides together, pin the shirt front to the shirt back along the shoulders and sides. Sew the shoulder seam 5½", 6¼", 7" (14, 15.9, 17.8 cm) from the edge on each side of the shirt. Each side seam should start down 8½", 9¼", 10" (21.6, 23.5, 25.4 cm) and go to the bottom edge of the shirt.

② **HEM THE SLEEVES** Fold the edge of the sleeve opening ¼" (6 mm), then ¼" (6 mm) more to finish the sleeve edge. Sew around the sleeve.

At the bottom edge of the hemmed sleeve opening, add a couple of horizontal rows of back and forth stitching (a bar tack) to reinforce seam.

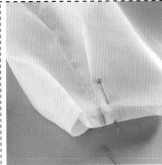

③ **PLEAT THE SLEEVE**
To give the sleeve shape and the shoulder profile some contour, pinch 1" (2.5 cm) of fabric and fold it toward the shoulder seam as shown. Pin to hold. Repeat on the other side of the shoulder seam, pinching and folding another pleat toward the shoulder seam. Pin to hold. If you want a simpler, straighter look, skip the pleated sleeve Steps altogether.

④ **STITCH THE PLEAT**
Sew across the top of the pleat to secure. Try to follow the same stitching line as was used in Step 2 to hem the sleeve.

⑤ **FINISH THE NECK**
Use the same double ¼" (6 mm) roll fold that you used to finish the sleeves in Step 2 to now finish the neck. Reinforce the hem/seam at the end of the neck opening with bar tacks as shown.

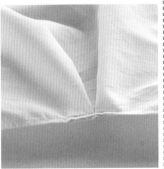

⑥ **PLEAT THE BACK**
Use the same pleating technique used at the shoulder in Step 3 on the back of the neck. Find the center point of the back and fold two 1" (2.5 cm) pleats inward toward it along the back neckline edge. Sew to secure running the stitching along the neckline hem stitching completed in Step 5.

⑦ **ACCORDIAN THE NECK**
Find the center front of the shirt along the top edge. Begin at the neckline, fold the edge down ½" (1.3 cm) toward the inside, then fold back ½" (1.3 cm) toward the outside. Fold again ½" (1.3 cm) toward the inside, alternating back and forth in accordion folds until you have a small stack of four folds with your last fold being toward the back. You will actually accordian back and forth 7 times to get a visible stack of 4 folds. Pin to hold.

⑧ **SEW THE FOLD**
With a needle and doubled thread, sew through the stack of folds several stitches to secure. With the same thread, attach a fancy button to the fold to cover the stitching and add some permanent jewelry to your neckline.

Foldover CROSSBODY

This crossbody bag crosses some boundaries. It lets you play with a lot of different materials, both raw and refined, to make an artisanal bag that uses traditional sewing to jump beyond the traditional.

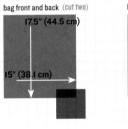

Size of bag folded over 14" wide x 11" tall x 4" deep (35.6 x 27.9 x 10.2 cm) (not including strap)

MATERIALS

½ yard (45.7 cm) black heavyweight canvas

½ yard (45.7 cm) colored heavyweight canvas for lining

piece of deerskin approximately 12" x 15" (30.5 x 38.1 cm) for bag bottom, another piece 6" x 12" (15.2 x 30.5 cm) for the optional strap

a small 8" x 10" (20.3 x 25.4 cm) piece of dark brown leather

magnetic snaps

2 opening "O" rings

2 swivel snap hooks

1 ½ yards (1.4 m) of 1-inch (2.5 cm) wide cotton, linen or hemp webbing for shoulder strap

TOOLS

sewing kit (see page 15)

leather sewing needle (for sewing machine)

scotch or masking tape

tissue paper

pencil

optional: screwdriver

MEASURE & CUT

bag front and back (cut two)

17.5" (44.5 cm)

15" (38.1 cm)

lining front and back (cut two)

16" (40.6 cm)

14.5" (36.8 cm)

deerskin bottom (cut one)

12" (30.5 cm)

15" (38.1 cm)

leather tabs

2.5" x 5" (6.4 x 12.7 cm) (cut one)

1" x 3" (2.5 x 7.6 cm) (cut two)

optional deerskin top strap (cut one)

5" x 18" (12.7 x 45.7 cm)

SOME TIPS FOR SEWING LEATHER

Most home sewing machines do a wonderful job of sewing leather once you have the machine needle made for sewing leather (they have a cutting tip to slice through the leather). The only problem I sometimes encounter is that the leather's surface can be a tad "sticky" so the pressure foot doesn't slide over it smoothly and the material doesn't properly feed through the machine resulting in bunched up stitches. I have found that laying a piece of thin tissue paper over the seam or top-stitching you want to sew, allows the machine to glide happily over the leather and make a very nice row of stitches. The material just tears away from the stitching when done. Tape (scotch or masking) works better than pins to temporarily secure leather. Just don't sew over the tape as it can be hard to remove from stitches.

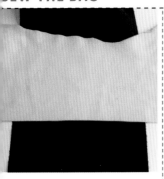

1 DEERSKIN Sew the outside bag pieces, right sides together, along the bottom (short) side with a ½" (1.3 cm) seam. Lay the piece flat, right side up. Lay the piece of deerskin centered in the middle of the outside canvas piece lining up the outside edges. Pin or tape in place. Sew along the outside edge of the deerskin, then add another row of top-stitching about ¼" (6 mm) in from the first.

2 SIDE SEAMS Fold this assembled piece in half, right sides together, down the center of the deerskin. Line-up the top and the side edges to make the front and back of the bag. Pin and sew the two side seams. Your machine should handle the deerskin easily because your pressure foot will be sliding across fabric not leather.

3 BOTTOM GUSSET At the corners, grab and spread the fabric out laterally so the point turns in the opposite direction as shown to make the bottom gusset. (See the bag on page 55 for another view of how this works). Stitch a horizontal seam across the gusset about 2" (5.1 cm) from the point. Repeat on the opposite corner. Turn the bag right side out.

This gusset will give the bottom of the bag its 3-dimensional shape and create a flat bottom that it can sit on. Plus, it obviously looks cool.

4 MAKE THE LINING Put the two pieces of the lining together and sew seams along the two sides and the bottom. Pull the fabric laterally to separate the front piece from the back so the corner points in the opposite direction as shown. Mark a point up 2" (5.1 cm) from the point of the corner, and sew a horizontal line across. Repeat this gusset on the other bottom corner.

5 ATTACH THE LINING With the lining still inside-out, place the outer bag inside the lining so the right sides are together as shown. Line up the top edges and the side seams. Pin and sew a ½" (1.3 cm) seam around the top leaving a 4" (10.2 cm) gap to turn the bag. Turn the bag through the gap so the outer piece is right side out and the lining inside. Stuff the bottom of the lining

to the bottom of the bag. Since the lining is a little shorter than the outside of the bag, a little of the outside fabric will roll down to the inside. Pin the lining and the outside of the bag together at the top, closing the gap through which you turned the bag.

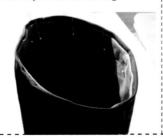

6 STITCH THE TOP EDGE Sew two rows of top-stitching at the top of the bag, one ⅛" (3 mm) from the edge and the other ⅜" (9.5 mm). Use contrasting thread for an edgier look.

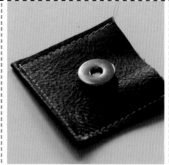

(7) **INSTALL THE SNAP**

Following manufacturer's instructions, position the female part of the magnetic snap near the bottom edge of the leather tab piece. Its center should be about 1 ¼" (3.2 cm) away from the edge. Use the snap itself to mark the leather where the two prongs will go through. Carefully cut two small slices in the leather with the tip of your scissors and insert the prongs.

(8) **SECURE THE SNAP**

On the wrong side of the leather tab, fit the stabilizing metal disk over the protruding prongs. Bend the prongs down to lock the disk in place using your thumb or the flat side of a screwdriver.

(9) **FINISH THE TAB**

Fold the leather tab in half, with wrong sides together, lining up the edges. Sew along the sides and the bottom ⅛" (3 mm) in from the edge. Leave the top of the tab open as shown.

(10) **SEW ON THE TAB**

Position the tab in the center of the bag. The un-sewn end of the tab should sit about ½" (1.3 cm) in from the edge of the bag. Tape to hold, then stitch across the tab to secure it following exactly along the lines of top-stitching from Step 7.

(11) **MARK POSITION**

The easiest way to mark the position of the second/bottom half of the magnetic snap, is to snap it together with the top half, fold down the top of the bag so the tab is positioned where it will be when the bag is closed, and mark the position of the two prongs of the bottom piece as shown. Then, with the tip of your scissors, snip two tiny slots in the fabric layers to allow the prongs to go through.

(12) **INSTALL THE SNAP**

Position the stabilizing metal disk on the prongs as shown and repeat the same process as illustrated in Step 9.

(13) **FINISH THE SNAP**

Cut a 2" (5.1 cm) circle of leather to use to cover the backside of the snap. Position it on the inside of the bag centered over the metal disk. Tape to hold. On the outside of the bag, use the snap as a convenient guide to sew a perfect circle an even distance around the outside of the snap as shown.

This leather cover on the inside keeps the metal disk and prongs from being exposed and causing trouble for the contents of the bag.

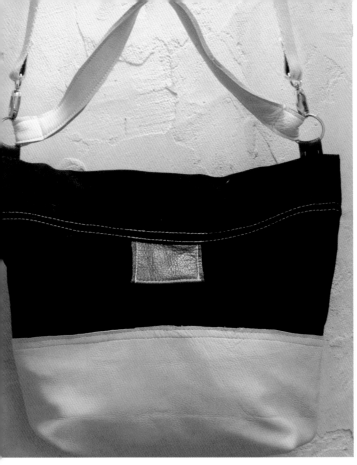

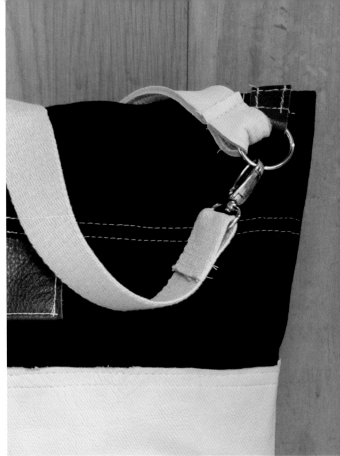

(14) **STRAP HOLDERS**
These tabs and rings are designed to be flexible so you can change your strap/handle options. The "O" ring opens to allow you to add the optional top handle on the purse. The longer crossbody strap has swivel snap hooks to snap on to the same "O" rings. To make the tab, fold the smaller strip of dark leather in half and slip the "O" ring in the middle. Sew two rows of stitching, about 1" (2.5 cm) long, along the edges of the leather as shown. Make two.

(15) **ADD THE STRAP TABS**
Position the strap tab, with the ring up, about 1" (2.5 cm) in from the edge on the back side of the bag. Place the bottom edge of the tab about 4" (10.2 cm) down from the bag's top edge. Sew two rows of stitching horizontally across the tab, once at the bottom edge of the tab and another that crosses the vertical stitching along the top edge.

(16) **HANDLE AND STRAP** To make the handle, fold the leather in half the long way to make a double-thick strap 2 ½" x 18" (6.4 x 45.7 cm). Sew both the folded and the raw edges of the strap closed about ¼" (6 mm) in from the edge. Using sharp scissors, cut the edges of the strap to about ⅛" (3 mm) from the stitching to neaten up the sides. Fold the ends of the strap over 1" to 1 ½" (2.5 to 3.8 cm)to make the end loop. Sew horizontally across the strap about ¼" (6 mm) away from

the raw edge to close the loop. Repeat on the opposite end. Open the "O" ring, insert the metal end through the leather loop, and close the "O" ring to secure.

To make the crossbody strap, cut a 42" (106.7 cm) length of webbing. Slide a swivel snap hook over the end and fold up about 1 ½" (3.8 cm) to make a loop. Sew two rows of stitching horizontally across strap to secure. Snap the swivel hook onto the bag's "O" ring. Repeat on the opposite strap end to complete.

Urban DUFFEL

Duffels shouldn't just be for sailors and yoga mats anymore. They have a sleek, natural nautical attitude that brings a little extra dash to even the most mundane adventure.

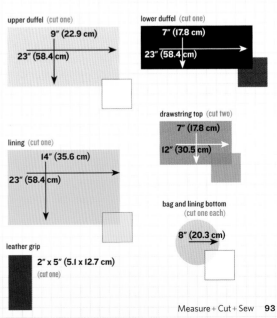

EASY HARD
gauge of difficulty

18" high x 8" (45.7 x 20.3 cm) across (not including strap)

MATERIALS

heavyweight canvas
½ yard (45.7 cm) natural
¼ yard (22.9 cm) yellow or
black for accent
½ yard (45.7 cm) bright
color for interior

¼ yard (22.9 cm) of natural
linen or heavyweight cotton
ticking for duffel top

1 yard (91.4 cm) heavy-
weight cotton, linen or
hemp 1-inch (2.5 cm) wide
webbing

4" x 8" (10.2 x 20.3 cm)
piece of brown leather for
strap grip

1 yard (91.4 cm) of nylon
cord for drawstring closure

TOOLS

sewing kit (see page 15)

8" (20.3 cm) salad plate for
circle template

MEASURE & CUT

upper duffel (cut one)

9" (22.9 cm)

23" (58.4 cm)

lower duffel (cut one)

7" (17.8 cm)

23" (58.4 cm)

lining (cut one)

14" (35.6 cm)

23" (58.4 cm)

drawstring top (cut two)

7" (17.8 cm)

12" (30.5 cm)

bag and lining bottom
(cut one each)

8" (20.3 cm)

leather grip

2" x 5" (5.1 x 12.7 cm)
(cut one)

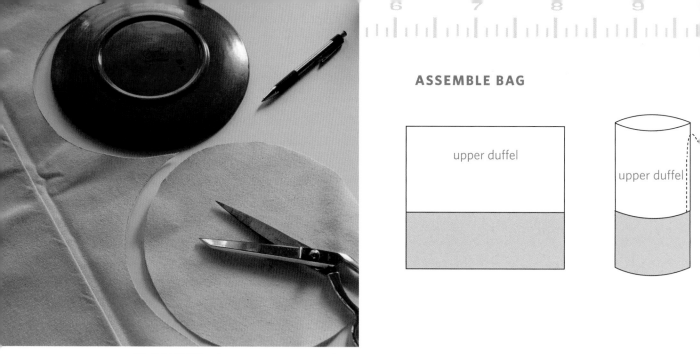

ASSEMBLE BAG

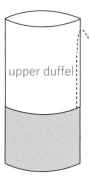

upper duffel

upper duffel

1 BASIC ASSEMBLY

Put together the natural colored upper duffel piece with the black lower duffel section along the long sides with right sides together. Pin and sew. Fold this composite piece in half lining up the edges. Pin and sew the back seam to make this a tube. Begin pinning the lower duffel edge to the circular bottom piece with right sides together. Work your way around the outside edge, using a lot of pins to ease the fabric around the arc as shown.

2 SEW BOTTOM AND SIDE

Continue working around the circle, easing the fabric in as you go, until you reach the side seam.

3 ADD THE STRAP

Slip the end of a 32" (81.3 cm) piece of webbing between the sides and the bottom piece at the side seam. The end of the strap should stick out the bottom as shown. Sew carefully around the circular bottom ½" (1.3 cm) from the edge.

4 TOP STITCH THE SEAMS

With the right sides facing out, stitch around the outside of the lower (black) duffel piece just where it hits the bottom circle as shown here.

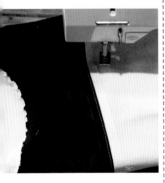   

5 MORE TOPSTITCHING

Also topstitch two rows on either side of the seam where the upper and lower duffel sections meet. This stitching is mostly decorative though it gives the middle of the bag a little more structural rigidity. The stitching should be about ⅛" (3 mm) on either side of the seam.

6 SEW THE LINING

Fold the lining piece in half and with right sides together, pin then sew the back seam as in Step 1. Pin the bottom circular piece to the main body piece as in Steps 1 and 2 above. Sew. Turn the outside of the duffel right side out, and the lining piece wrong side out. Now stuff the lining inside the outer duffel, lining up the back seams and making sure the lining is all the way to the bottom. Trim any excess off the top of the lining so the tops of both lining and outer bag are even. Pin to hold.

7 ASSEMBLE GATHERED TOP

Sew together the two linen pieces that will make the gathered top. Sew the side seams leaving the top edge open about 1" (2.5 cm) as shown.

8 FINISH GATHERED TOP

Fold down the top edge of the linen piece ½" (1.3 cm) then fold this folded edge down ½" (1.3 cm) more to make a casing for the drawstrings. There will be four openings in the casing, 2 at each side. These will allow the drawstring ends to emerge. Pin and sew the casing.

⑨ **CUT THE LEATHER** Cut the leather piece for the strap grip out of a scrap of cowhide. This piece has to be wide enough to fold over the strap webbing with an additional ½" (1.3 cm) for the seam, but the length can be anything from 6" to 9" (15.2 to 22.9 cm), depending on preference.

⑩ **MAKE THE GRIP** Fold the leather in half the long way. Sew a seam about ¼" (6 mm) from the raw edge. Thread the strap through the end and out the other side. Turn the grip so the seam is toward the back.

⑪ **ATTACH THE STRAP** With the grip on the strap, pin the loose end of the strap webbing to the top edge of the duffel at the seam. Make sure the strap is straight with no twists before sewing across the strap horizontally to secure.

⑫ **ATTACH THE TOP** Slide the top piece created in Step 8 over the outside of the duffel with right sides together. Line up the side seam with the duffel's side seams. Line up the top edges. Pin then sew all the way around the duffel's top opening.

⑬ **PULL UP THE TOP** Turn up the top piece as shown, then stuff it into the interior of the duffel smoothing the seam all around the top edge.

⑭ **FINISH THE EDGE** Pin the linen top piece down along the top edge of the duffel as shown. Make sure there are no tucks, gathers, or creases.

⑮ **TOPSTITCH** Sew a round of top-stitching about ½" (1.3 cm) down from the top edge of the duffel. This seats the linen gathered top down in the duffel making both a sturdier and a more finished-looking edge. The strap that you positioned in Step 11 comes straight out the top of the seam and falls nicely down the back of the duffel.

⑯ **ADD DRAWSTRINGS** Cut two pieces of cord 30" (76.2 cm) each. Attach a safety pin to one end and feed the cord through the hole left in the top casing. Work the cord all the way around the casing 360 degrees to come back out of the hole on the same side of as where it went in. Now attach the pin to the other length of cord, and thread it through the same casing but starting on the opposite side of the duffel as shown. Even out the ends, tie into a knot, and cut off the excess.

Beyond Measure QUILT

Can you handle making it up as you go along? Some of the best things in life don't start with a rule book. This soft and lovely quilt is a study in improv, just adding one thing at a time without measuring or too much planning.

Approximate size 40" x 40" (101.6 x 101.6 cm) (size varies)

MATERIALS

¼ yard (22.9 cm) or smaller scraps of a dozen calico prints in similar colors, here greens, blues, and aquas

1 yard (91.4 cm) of natural cotton muslin

¾ yard (68.6 cm) of natural linen

1 ½ yards (1.4 m) of cotton calico for backing

bamboo or cotton quilt batting

TOOLS

sewing kit *(see page 15)*

MEASURE & CUT

This project is a cut as you go project. See the basics on the next page. Note that I used the *wrong* sides of the calico prints because I liked how the colors and patterns were more muted on the back side. The various fabrics harmonize effortlessly giving the quilt a soft, lived-in, vintage look.

USE ¼" (6 MM) SEAMS FOR PIECING FABR

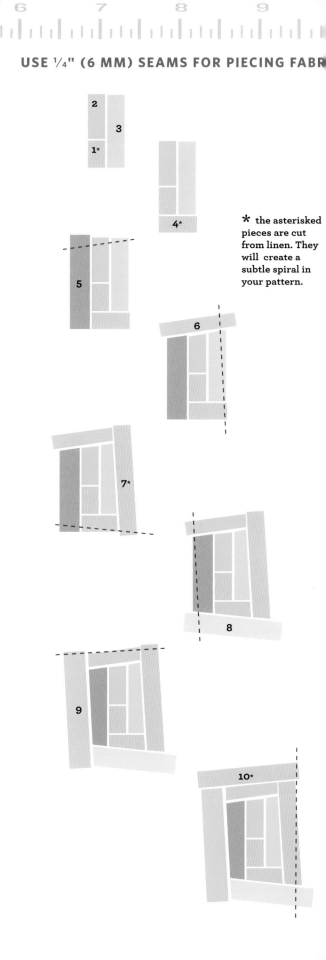

* the asterisked pieces are cut from linen. They will create a subtle spiral in your pattern.

MAKE THE CUT Cut calico and linen in strips varying between 2″ and 3½″ (5.1 and 8.9 cm) wide. They needn't be perfect. Cut as you go so you can choose the fabric color and pattern that looks best, and, bonus, you won't waste fabric by cutting a bunch of stuff ahead of time that you never use!

length and width varies

Quilt strips
Cut-as-you-go

Cut many strips of calico in widths 2" to 3½ " (5.1 to 8.9 cm) wide. The length is dependent on the pattern you are building on. See illustrations and photos at right to get the hang of it.

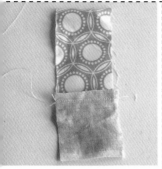

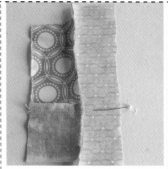

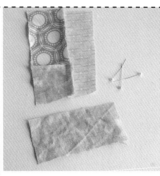

(1) **THE FIRST PIECES**
Cut a square of natural linen about 2″ (5.1 cm) to begin. Cut a strip out of calico that is about the same width and at least twice as long. Sew the two pieces together as shown with a ¼″ (6 mm) seam. **NOTE:** all seams for the piecing portion of this quilt project are ¼″ (6 mm).

(2) **ADD THE 3RD PIECE**
Cut another strip of calico 2″ to 3″ (5.1 to 7.6 cm) wide and long enough to extend the length of the piece from Step 1. Pin and sew as shown.

(3) **TRIM THE EDGES** Trim the edges of the sewn pieces from the last two Steps. The trimmed edge needs to be even, but it can be at an angle. This angling as you go along makes for a more interesting pieced design. The best way is to generally angle it one way on one round then angle it the other direction the next time around so your finished piece is roughly square and not too crooked.

(4) **ADD LINEN PIECE**
There is a very subtle spiral that runs through this pieced design that is made by adding a linen section every fourth piece. This linen piece will always touch another linen piece and is always the first piece in each "round" as you add pieces while working clockwise around the center. Add the linen piece onto the bottom of your design as shown.

(5) **TRIM THE EDGES** Trim the over-long edges off the recently added piece in line with the previous pieces as shown.

(6) **KEEP ADDING PIECES**
Now add the next piece to the existing design. Pin and sew. Remember, you are adding pieces by moving around in a clockwise direction and adding a linen piece every fourth step.

(7) **KEEP IT LINEAR**
Use a straightedge to scribe a line that evens up the edges. Angled cuts keep things interesting.
Note how the linen spirals through the design. Also note how the angled lines give the overall design more movement and attitude. To keep it from getting impossibly crooked, angle the pieces on any given

sides in one direction, then angle the next round on that same side in the opposite direction to keep things square. Pardon me for repeating myself about this, but it is really the *only* slightly complex thing about this piecing process . . .

⑧ FINISHED DESIGN

Keep adding calico strips until the pieced design is somewhere around 19" (48.3 cm) square. Give it a light pressing with an iron to flatten out the piece. Now is the time to square up the edges a bit so the design is easier to add the wide bands of muslin and linen and make a nice and neat square quilt.

⑨ FOLD THE PIECE IN HALF

At this point, the ends and edges will be pretty far out of whack. Don't despair, this is no problem! First fold the piece in half, aligning the edges as best you can.

⑩ FOLD AGAIN

Now fold the piece in quarters, again aligning the edges as well as you can given the ad hoc nature of the piece. Lay a ruler at right angles to the folded edge and mark a straight line. Cut along the line to square. Lay the ruler on the other edge, perpendicular to the fold, mark then cut that side straight as well. (You can use a square or angle tool for this, too.) This piece should now unfold into a rough square or rectangle.

⑪ ADD THE BACKGROUND

There are no rules about an exact size for this quilt or even whether it need be perfectly square. Add 8" or 9"-wide (20.3 or 22.9 cm) side panels of muslin that run the length of the sides of the pieced design. You can continue using the ¼" (6 mm) seam here. Once you've added the side pieces, add top and bottom muslin pieces, also 8" or 9" wide (20.3 or 22.9 cm), that run the width of the pieced design plus the newly-added side panels.

⑫ ADD LINEN FRAME

Add a band of linen that is about 4" (10.2 cm) wide and runs the full height on both sides. Add the same 4" (10.2 cm) wide bands to the top and bottom running the full width of the pieced design, muslin band and linen band as well. Once the front is complete, lay down first a large piece of calico for the quilt back, wrong side up. It should be at least 3" (7.6 cm) bigger on all edges than the quilt top. Then lay down a layer of quilt batting, then the

quilt top, right side up. Trim away any quilt batting so its even with the edge of the quilt top. Leave the overhang on the quilt back. Begin "quilting" the pieces together by sewing slightly meandering lines of stitching from one end of the quilt to the other. Start with a line of stitching that goes down the center of the quilt. Then sew another line perpendicular to this first that goes horizontally through the center. Work out from these two center lines adding stitching every 3" (7.6 cm) or so. (See Quilting 101 on the opposite page)

⑬ FINISH THE EDGE

Once all the rows of quilting stitching are complete, its time to finish the edge. Trim the backing fabric so it extends 1½" (3.8 cm) beyond the quilted piece all the way around. Starting on one side, fold the backing over ½" (1.3 cm), then roll it over another ½" (1.3 cm). The final ½" (1.3 cm) roll folds over the edge of the quilted piece. Pin to hold. Work your way down both sides of the quilt.

⑭ TOPSTITCH THE EDGE

Topstitch along the rolled/folded edge of the quilt first on the sides, then roll/fold the top and bottom edges. Pin then sew to finish the quilt.

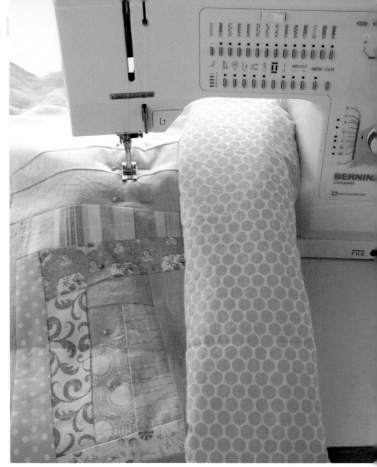

MUSLIN SIDE PANELS LONG
Cut **two** of muslin for sides

MUSLIN SIDE PANELS SHORT
Cut **two** of muslin for sides

LINEN SIDE PANELS LONG
Cut **two** of linen for sides

LINEN SIDE PANELS SHORT
Cut **two** of linen for sides

QUILT BACKING
Cut **one** of calico 3" (7.6 cm)
larger on each side than quilt front

QUILTING 101

This quilt is meant to have imperfect quilting. Meandering, wonky, curvy. Its easier and more lively that way. You want rows that are generally moving from one edge of the quilt to the other, but if they weave and wiggle a little, that is absolutely fine. Here's how to do it:

START WITH A ROW OF PINS down the center of the quilt. Roll the side of the quilt that is on the right into a nice bundle (as shown above right) so it fits nicely into the sewing machine. Sew this vertical row, then sew another row of stitching about 3" (7.6 cm) to the right of this center row. Add another row of stitching 3" (7.6 cm) to the left of the original row.

TURN THE QUILT 90 DEGREES, using the same rolling up technique as before to make the quilt more maneuverable, sew a row of stitching down the center of the quilt that runs perpendicular to the first rows. Then add more rows as before, one 3" (7.6 cm) to the left, the other 3" (7.6 cm) to the right.

MAKE THE WIDE GRID Continue working outward in both directions adding new rows of stitching every 3" (7.6 cm) until the entire quilt is covered with this widely-spaced grid.

FILL IN THE LINES. Add 2 rows of stitching, approximately evenly spaced, between each of the rows so that the final quilting pattern is approximately a 1" (2.5 cm) grid. If stitching wanders too close to its neighbor somewhere, or veers away, that is just fine. It gives the quilt a unique fingerprint that gives it character.

Crowns & Laurels BABY HATS

These hats start with the simplest idea. Then comes a bauble or flourish to make them more colorful and cuter, more frolicsome and fun. Use these as simple inspiration, then get playful, even silly, with concoctions of your own.

Hat circumference: Newborn 13″ (33 cm), 3–6 months 15″ (38.1 cm), 6–12 months 17″ (43.2 cm)

MATERIALS

¼ yard (22.9 cm) each of cotton knit for the inside and outside of the hat

scraps, jelly roll, or fat squares of calico cotton to add colorful accents

(for bauble crown hat) a tiny bit of loose batting, stuffing, or a few cotton balls

(for ribbon tuftie hat) ½ yard (45.7 cm) grosgrain ribbon

TOOLS

sewing kit (see page 15)

small juice or water glass for circle template

MEASURE & CUT

hat outside (cut one)

14″, 16″, 18″ (35.6, 40.6, 45.7 cm)

8″, 9″, 9.5″ (20.3, 22.9, 24.1 cm)

✂ cut so stretch is across not up and down

hat inside (cut one)

same as above

Sizing for small, medium, large

① **INNER AND OUTER HAT**
Fold the inner and the outer pieces for the hat in half along the long edge. Pin and sew a ½" (1.3 cm) back seam on each.

② **ASSEMBLE HAT**
Turn the inner hat piece right side out. Slide the inner hat piece into the outer hat piece so right sides are together and the back seams line up. Pin the two pieces together and sew around the top edge.

③ **TURN HAT**
Turn the sewn piece so it is right side out with the outer hat on the outside and the lining on the inside. Fold up the seamed edge at the bottom to make the hat's cuff.

④ **TOP EDGE**
Line up the top edges of the outer hat and the lining. Pin the outer to the inner hat and sew around the upper edge.

⑤ **MAKE CROWN POINTS**
Cut four pieces of scrap calico 2 ½" x 5 ½" (6.4 x 14 cm). Fold in half the long way and mark the center of the folded edge. Stitch an angled line from the bottom corner to the marked point. Pivot on the point and then sew another angled line to the other corner. Trim and turn right side out to make a point.

⑥ **CUSTOMIZE THE TOP**
Turn the hat inside out and lay flat with the seam up. Fold the hat so the seam is in the center. Pin at the seam and sew 1" (2.5 cm) down to make two "pockets" on either side of the seam as shown.

⑦ **FOUR SECTIONS**
Fold each of those two pockets the opposite direction, pin in the center to make two more pocket on each side for a total of 4. Now place the crown points you made in Step 5 in each pocket, insert the points facing down as shown.

⑧ **SEW THE TOP**
Pin each of the crown points in place. Sew across the top of each of the pockets to secure the crown points and sew closed the top of the hat. Complete all four to finish the hat. Turn the hat right side out and fold up the bottom cuff to finish.

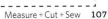

SEW THE BAUBLE HAT

① CUT THE CIRCLES For the bauble hat, cut 4 circles of calico fabric preferably each in a different color/print. The exact size of the circle isn't too important. Here a small water glass serves as the perfect template to trace around before cutting.

② FILL WITH STUFFING Add a wad of stuffing about the size of a cherry or larger to the center of the fabric circle.

③ MAKE A BUNDLE Gather up all the edges into a little bundle and tie with a piece of thread. Or, alternatively, pin the bundle tightly at the base of the ball, then sew across to secure.

④ ATTACH THE BAUBLES Assemble the hat as in Steps I through 4 on the preceding pages then substitute the four baubles you just made for the four crown points in Steps 6, 7, and 8.

SEW THE LAUREL & RIBBON TUFTIE HATS

   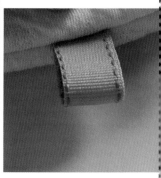

① MAKE THE LAURELS Cut circles that are approximately 2½" to 3" (6.4 to 7.6 cm) in diameter. A juice or water glass makes a great tracing template. These can be made from the same fabric or you can use a couple different colors/prints. Fold the circle in half, cut the folded edge so you have two half circles. Sew a ½" (1.3 cm) seam around the circle's arc leaving the bottom open. Trim the edge back to about ¼" (6 mm) and clip the arc with the scissor tips. Turn right side out. Make four or five.

② POSITION AND PIN Follow Steps 1-4 on the preceding pages to make the hat base. With the hat inside out, line up the semi-circles along the top inside edge with the circles facing downward as shown. Fit them across the entire width of the hat, overlapping them a little if need be. Pin to secure.

③ SEW THE HAT CLOSED Sew across the top of the hat to close the top and secure the laurels. Turn the hat right-side out and turn up the cuff to expose the colorful lining.

④ OPTIONS! This same technique works for other embellishments like these pieces of ribbon folded in two and spaced out across the top of the hat. Add them as described in the preceding Steps.

Playtime TEEPEE

What kid hasn't made a fort or tent or secret hiding place from a blanket? This simple project takes it a step further making a beautiful teepee from a single twin-sized sheet. And it does it using just one, *one*, diagonal cut!

Teepee is approximately 45" square at the base x 65" tall
(114.3 x 165.1 cm)

MATERIALS

one twin-sized flat sheet
(68" x 96" [172.7 x 243.8
cm])

¾ yard (68.6 cm) of ribbon
for flap ties

four 8-foot tall (2.4 m),
¾-inch (1.9 cm) bamboo
poles (available at hardware
stores and garden centers)

1 yard (91.4 cm) or two of
soft rope or twill tape to tie
together the bamboo poles

optional self-adhesive
hook-and-loop tape

TOOLS

sewing kit *(see page 15)*

tape measure, masking
tape, or long section of
ribbon to use as guide for
lengthy diagonal cut

MEASURE & CUT

The entire teepee is cut
from one twin flat sheet.
The sheet is folded in
fourths and then only one
diagonal cut is required to
make all the pieces for the
iconic teepee structure. This
piece of ribbon stretched
from corner to diagonal
corner is an easy way to
indicate the cutting line to
make all the teepee pieces.

68" (172.7 cm)

96" (243.8 cm)

front flap

teepee back

front flap

teepee side

teepee side

Here are the pieces that come out of the single twin-sized sheet

fold twin sheet in half, then in half again

68" (172.

24" (61 cm)

Two simple folds, in half then in half again, and one diagonal cut from corner to corner.

All the pieces you need for the teepee, 3 full triangles and 2 half triangles

Cut through all four layers of your double folded sheet.

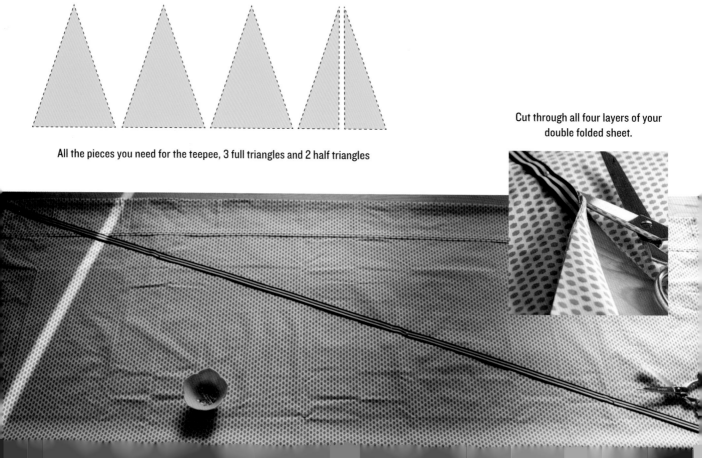

(1) PIECE TOGETHER

Sew together the three full triangles along the vertical edges with a ½" (1.3 cm) seam. Sew one of the half triangles on each side of those 3 full triangles. These will eventually be the door flaps.

(2) CUT OFF THE TOP

Once the triangles are all pieced together, cut off the top 7" (17.8 cm) as shown. Measure down 7" (17.8 cm) at every seam, mark, then cut from point to marked point across all the teepee panels.

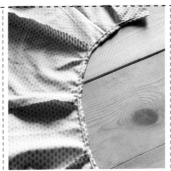

(3) FINISH THE TOP EDGE

Finish the newly-cut edge by folding it down ¼" (6 mm), then rolling that fold down ¼" (6 mm) more.

(4) MAKE THE DOOR

FLAP The original fold made to the sheet brought the wide finished hem on one end to meet the narrow finished hem on the other. These finished hems are along the straight edge of the two half triangles that will now make the flap. No need to finish these front edges, as the purchased sheet has already done the work for you. Lap the wide hem over the narrow, pin together, and sew down about 18" (45.7 cm) from the top.

(5) POLE POCKETS

You will need to sew a wide tube/pocket down the four corners of the teepee to hold the bamboo poles. The exact size can vary depending on the thickness of the poles, however a 1½" (3.8 cm) pole pocket should suffice for a ½" to 1" (1.3 to 2.5 cm) pole. Make it easy to create a consistent width pocket by adding a piece of tape on your sewing machine to use as a guide. (I used red tape here).

(6) FINISH POCKETS

Sew the bottom edge of the pole pocket to close it so the pole won't slip through the end. Repeat on all four pole pockets.

(7) FLAP TIES

Cut two pieces of ribbon 12" (30.5 cm) long. Position one piece on the inside of the door flap about 10" to 12" (25.4 to 30.5 cm) down from the flap opening. Sew around the edge of the ribbon to secure. Repeat on the opposite flap. If you'd like, you can sew ties on the bottom edge of the teepee flaps to close them more completely.

(8) TIE THE POLES

Insert the poles. Use a piece of soft rope or a twill tape to tie the four poles together at the top. Weave the tie in and out of the poles to steady and bring them together where they naturally cross right above the fabric.

NOTE: If you find the fabric slipping down the poles at the top, you can add a dot of self-adhesive hook-and-loop tape to the inside edge of the pole pocket top and to the bamboo pole to hold in place.

Fuzzy Forest FRIENDS

It's amazing how little it takes to turn a few scraps of cloth and a bit of imagination into a menagerie of very huggable, just-my-size companions. Here are the simple instructions to make an owl, a bunny, and a little fox.

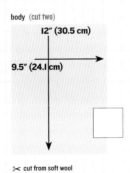

EASY HARD

gauge of difficulty

Each stuffed animal is approximately 9.5″ x 12″ (24.1 x 30.5 cm) (excluding ears and feet)

MATERIALS

each stuffed animal requires about ¼ yard (22.9 cm) of woolen fabric for the body. It can be 100% wool flannel, or felted wool from an old sweater

scraps of wool or wool felt for the eyes, nose, toes, ears, etc

polyester, cotton or bamboo stuffing

coordinating thread

TOOLS

sewing kit *(see page 15)*

8″ (20.3 cm) salad plate for circle template (for the owl)

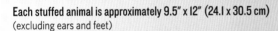

MEASURE & CUT

body (cut two)

12″ (30.5 cm)

9.5″ (24.1 cm)

✂ cut from soft wool

Each of the three creatures require the same sized cuts to make the back and front of the body. Dimensions shown here work for the owl, the fox, and the bunny. Only the colors and the embellishment details are different.

The detail sidebars on the following pages are just rough suggestions for features to use for the animals' faces and bodies. These are not cutting templates and are meant to just use as a guide.

FOX DETAILS

FACE

2-inch (5.1 cm) square cut diagonally

1-inch (2.5 cm) circles for eyes and nose

EARS

triangle about 3" wide by (7.6 x 12.7 cm) tall

triangle 1.5" wide by 2.5 (3.8 x 6.5 cm) tall

PAWS

oval about 3" wide by 1.5 (7.6 x 3.8 cm) tall cut in half

rectangle about 3" x 1.5 (7.6 x 3.8 cm)

1 MAKE A FACE

Cut the rectangles for the fox front and back. Cut a 2" (5.1 cm) square of white wool, then cut it along the diagonal. These are the cheeks/sides of the nose for the fox face. Position them on the background as shown. Add the two dark 1" (2.5 cm) circles on the top edge of the triangles as eyes and a brown 1" (2.5 cm) circle at the bottom edge of the triangles for the tip of the nose.

2 SEW IN PLACE

Use contrasting thread where possible to make the stitching more characterful–like white on dark elements and a bright orange on the light ones. Don't be afraid to make the stitching stand out by using multiple rows or using a tight zig-zag stitch, as shown here for the pupils of the eyes.

3 OUTLINE THE FACE

Sew an outline around the facial features to highlight them. Here I used a subtle and imprecise heart/arrowhead shape that outlined the basic geometry of the fox face. Repeat with 2 or 3 rows of stitching that follow the same general path to highlight the feature. The stitching looks better if it is **NOT** too perfect.

4 MAKE THE EARS

Cut four triangles in the same reddish brown wool as the body. Pile two on top of each other then sew a couple rows of contrasting stitching around the outside edge. Cut two smaller triangles in gray wool, line up one with the bottom edge of the sewn ear triangle and sew around the edge with a zig zag stitch in dark thread. Make two ears.

5 ATTACH THE EARS

Position the ears centered on the top edge about 2" or 3" (5.1 or 7.6 cm) apart and about ¼" (6 mm) down. Pin then sew along the edge with a straight stitch to secure.

6 MAKE THE PAWS

Cut out four small rectangles of dark brown wool. Stack two pieces together and sew around the outside edge (about ⅛" [3 mm] in) with two rows of stitching as shown. Cut an oval of white wool as wide as these rectangles. Cut the oval in half and place the cut edge along the bottom edge of the doubled rectangle. Sew on with wide zig zag stitch as shown. Make two paws. Position paws with the white part down on the bottom of the fox body almost to the outside edge. Attach as in Step 5.

7 BORDER STITCHING

Sew three rows of stitching around the outside of the fox front as shown. The stitching should be imperfect with a bit of meandering.

8 COMPLETE THE BODY

Stack the fox front on the fox back piece lining up the edges, with wrong sides together. Pin and sew a line of stitching about ⅛" to ¼" (3 to 6 mm) in from the edge. Leave a gap of about 2" (5.1 cm) on one side to use for stuffing. Fill the interior of the body with the stuffing of your choice through the gap left open. Once you are happy with the feel of the fox, pin the hole closed and continue the edge stitching to close.

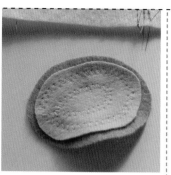

① ADD THE FACE

Cut two dark circles for eyes and a pink, slightly-rounded triangle for a nose. Sew the eyes in place with multiple intersecting lines of stitching as shown.

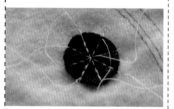

② NOSE AND MOUTH

Sew on the nose with a straight stitch, then add a bit of red zig-zagging to the center. "Draw" straight down from the nose with dark stitching to make the mouth detail as shown. Use 2 or 3 tight tows of stitching to make the detail visible. Then add a little horizontal, upward arc to suggest the bunny's mouth.

③ RABBITS FOOT

Cut two light brown circles, and two slightly smaller pink circles to make the feet.

Attach the pink smaller circle to the larger with two rows of zig-zag one within the other as shown. Cut the circles in half and attach the feet as was done for the fox.

BUNNY DETAILS

FACE

1" (2.5 cm) circles for eyes

rounded triangle about 1.5" (3.8 cm) across and 1" (2.5 cm) tall

OWL DETAILS

FACE

cut a small triangle for nose

¾" (1.9 cm) circles for pupil

2.5-inch (6.4 cm) circles for eye

④ BUNNY EARS

Cut two tall, rounded triangles out of the white wool. Sew them together along the outside edge. Cut a smaller rounded triangle in tan wool. Center it on the larger ear piece and sew a row of stitching along its outside edge. Fill in rows of stitching about ⅛" (3 mm) apart as shown. Red or pink thread works great for this. Make two ears. Attach to the front of the bunny as instructed for the fox.

⑤ FINISHED STITCHING

Add a tall narrow arch of stitching using pink thread that defines a basic bunny shape. Make three rows of imperfectly spaced stitching to add a bit of character to the face/body. For the outside border stitching, use a darker color thread like the dark blue-gray shown here. Try a zig-zag stitch to attach the back to the front for a little jauntier look. (see large photo on page 114) Fill and finish as for the fox.

EARS

rounded triangle about 2.5" (6.4 cm) wide and 4.5" (11.4 cm) tall

EARS

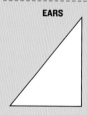

triangle about 3.5" (8.9 cm) wide and 3" (7.6 cm) tall

FEET

2.5" (6.4 cm) circle

3" (7.6 cm) circle

FEET

4" (10.2 cm) circle cut in half

THE OWL

Now that you have seen how these furry/feathery friends are put together, making the owl is a simple task. Use the photos of the finished owl as your guide and the owl detail information for a rough idea about the various pieces that you'll want to cut out. I used an 8" (20.3 cm) salad plate to cut the wings for the owl, and then stitched them on to the owl body with a few rows of zig-zag about 1" (2.5 cm) apart. The "talons" on the owls feet where just two diagonal lengths of stitching that divided each half-round foot into thirds.

OWL DETAILS

- - - - - - - - - - - - - - - - - -

8" (20.3 cm) circle (use salad plate as template) cut in half

Scrunchy Squishy BLOCKS

Of course these adorably soft and squishy blocks are made from simple squares, but that doesn't make it any less magical when they pop up into real live fun-to-stack toys. Half the joy in making them is picking the fabrics.

EASY HARD

gauge of difficulty

Makes 3 blocks, 4″, 6″, and 8″ (10.2, 15.2 , and 20.3 cm) square

MATERIALS

¼ yard (22.9 cm) or one fat quarter each of 6 different cotton calico prints

lots of stuffing
bamboo or cotton work best, but polyester is okay too

TOOLS

sewing kit (see page 15)

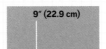

MEASURE & CUT

For each block, cut the squares out of six different calico prints

front, back, sides, top, bottom

9″ (22.9 cm)

9″ (22.9 cm)

front, back, sides, top, bottom

7″ (17.8 cm)

7″ (17.8 cm)

front, back, sides, top, bottom

5″ (12.7 cm)

5″ (12.7 cm)

A 90 degree plastic angle tool like the one above can make measuring, marking, and cutting the squares a breeze. I cut one square to the size needed for the block, then used it as the pattern to cut all the five others needed. Once you get the hang of cutting, assembling, and sewing the blocks, making a set of three takes no time at all.

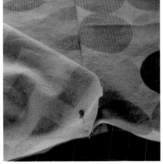

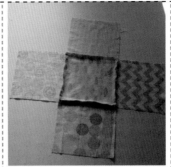

① HORIZONTAL SQUARES

Start with a center square, then attach a square, right sides together, along its left side using a ½" (1.3 cm) seam. Add another square on the other side of the center square.

② ADD VERTICAL SQUARES

Press the seams on the trio of horizontal squares outward. With right sides together, line up the fourth square along the edge of the center square. Begin pinning right at the seam from Step 1. Pin across the square to the other side, and stop right at the other seam. Sew between these two pins, stopping at the seams on either side as shown.

③ FINISH THE BASE

Add one more square along the top edge of the center square (which will become the bottom of your block). Follow the same directions, sewing only between the seams, as in Step 2. You will have a cross as shown here.

④ LINE UP THE EDGES

Fold the center/bottom piece along the diagonally bringing the edges of the two side pieces together as shown above. Line up these edges, right sides together, and pin.

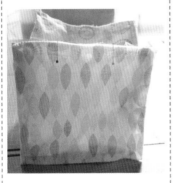

⑤ BRING THE SIDES UP

This angle shows how Step 4 creates the seam for the corner/side of the cube. Lay the cube flat again as in the previous step, and sew a ½" (1.3 cm) seam starting at the seam at the bottom edge, and ending ½" (1.3 cm) short of the top edge of the side pieces. Work around the entire cube, repeating the process to create all four corners of your cube, each time stopping short of the top edge. This will allow the top piece to fit on.

⑥ ADD THE TOP Pin the

top square along the top edges of your cube. Sew the four seams along the top edge one at a time, each time stopping at the top of the side seam. This makes a neat square corner. Leave a 3" (7.6 cm) section open along one of the seams to turn the cube right side out and to add the stuffing.

⑦ ADD THE STUFFING

Tear the stuffing into fluffy handfuls and stuff it through the hole left in the top edge. Work the filling down into the corners of the block and along the sides as you go so the final product will be fairly square and the edges not too rounded. A chopstick or knitting needle can help force the stuffing into the corners if need be.

⑧ CLOSE THE GAP

Once you are happy with the firmness of the block, pull the folded edges of the hole together and pin. Use a needle and doubled thread to make tiny stitches to pull the edges together and close the gap.

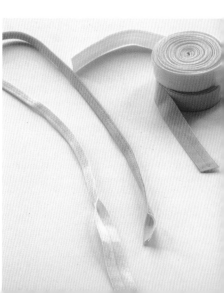

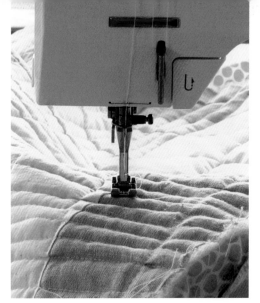

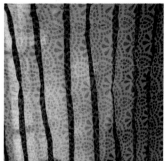
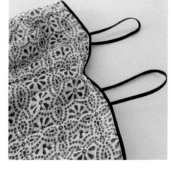

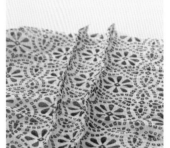
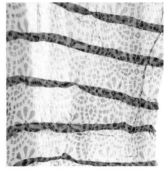
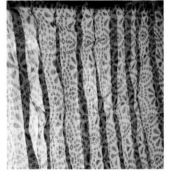

About the Author

Susan Wasinger designs houses, products, books, and magazines. Her work has been featured in *Metropolitan Home*, *Stitch*, *Natural Home*, and *Piecework* magazines, as well as on HGTV. She is the author of several Lark books, including *Eco Craft* (Lark, 2009), *The Feisty Stitcher* (Lark, 2010), *Artful Halloween* (Lark, 2012), and *Artful Christmas* (Lark, 2014). She lives in Boulder, Colorado.

Index